CRAZY
QUILTS

CRAZY QUILTS

A Beginner's Guide

BETTY FIKES PILLSBURY

Ohio University Press

Athens

Ohio University Press, Athens, Ohio 45701

ohioswallow.com

© 2016 by Ohio University Press

To obtain permission to quote, reprint, or otherwise reproduce or distribute material
from Ohio University Press publications, please contact our rights and permissions
department at (740) 593-1154 or (740) 593-4536 (fax).

Printed in the United States of America

Ohio University Press books are printed on acid-free paper ⊗ ™

26 25 24 23 22 21 20 19 18 17 16   5 4 3 2 1

Library of Congress Cataloging-in-Publication Data
Names: Pillsbury, Betty Fikes, 1962– author.
Title: Crazy quilts : a beginner's guide / Betty Fikes Pillsbury.
Description: Athens : Ohio University Press, [2016] | Includes
  bibliographical references and index.
Identifiers: LCCN 2016016832 | ISBN 9780821422137 (hc :acid-free paper) | ISBN
  9780821422144 (pb : acid-free paper) | ISBN 9780821445570 (pdf)
Subjects: LCSH: Quilting.
Classification: LCC TT835 .P556 2016 | DDC 746.46—dc23
LC record available at https://lccn.loc.gov/2016016832

THIS BOOK IS DEDICATED TO THE MEMORY OF
MY DEAR FRIEND, MARGARET "NUTMEG" BETZ.

SPECIAL THANKS TO CHERYL, ANN, AND AB

CONTENTS

1   HISTORICAL BACKGROUND   3

2   PERSONAL EXPERIENCE   16

3   BEGINNING YOUR CRAZY QUILT   35

4   STEM STITCH & VARIATIONS   59

5   BLANKET STITCH & VARIATIONS   65

6   HERRINGBONE STITCH & VARIATIONS   76

7   CRETAN STITCH & VARIATIONS   87

8   CHEVRON STITCH & VARIATIONS   94

9   COMBINATION STITCHES   99

10   FEATHERSTITCH & VARIATIONS   105

11   CHAIN STITCH & VARIATIONS   125

12   FRENCH KNOTS   138

13   BEADS   145

14   FABULOUS FLOWERS   158

GLOSSARY   173

RESOURCES   177

INDEX   179

CRAZY QUILTS

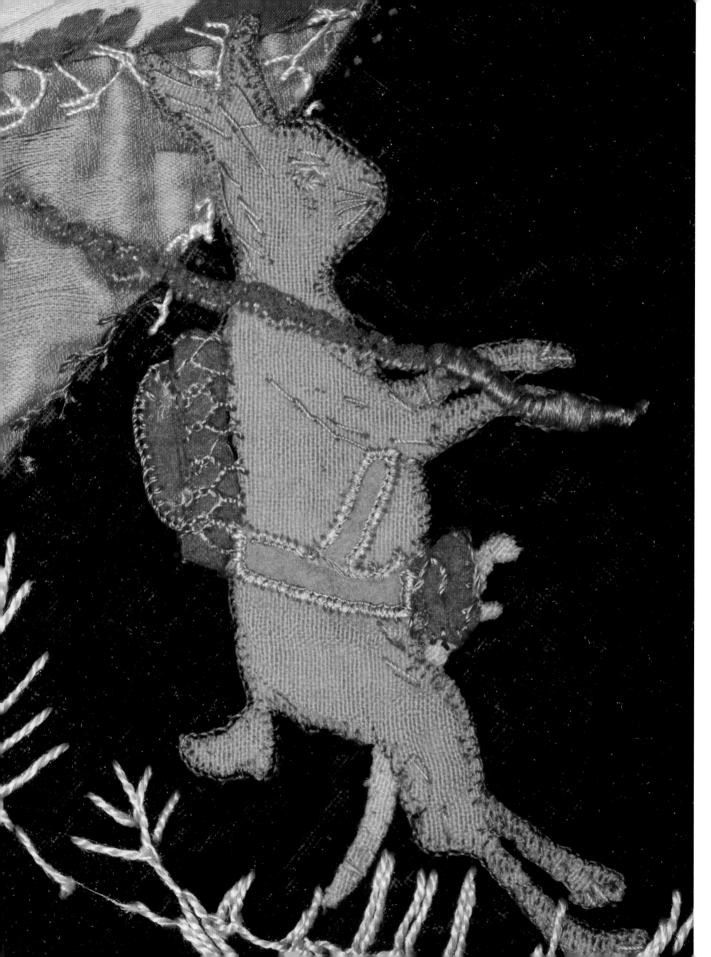

Historical Background

HAD ALREADY started a collection of Victorian crazy quilts and assorted ephemera when Penny McMorris' book, *Crazy Quilts*, captured my attention in regards to antique crazy quilts. With my intellectual curiosity honed by her scholarly work, I started delving into that grand era of crazy quilting myself, fascinated by the crazy quilts, their makers, and their stories.

During the years between 1880 and 1890, crazy quilts were at their height of popularity in the United States. Seemingly, every woman was working on one, or at least collecting silks, velvets, and damasks to make one. Her workbox probably held reels of silk thread and patterns garnered from the latest issue of *Harper's Bazaar* or *Godey's Lady's Book*. She may have talked her husband out of a necktie or handkerchief to include

1.1

in her quilt. Or, she might have decided to paint flowers onto taffeta to make her crazy quilt unique.

Crazy quilts are ornate, luscious, time-consuming, seemingly random works of textile art that provided Victorian women with a proper, accepted means to convey their thoughts and desires through an artistic outlet. By means of rich fabrics and silken threads, a woman could express her political, religious, social, and personal viewpoints. Perhaps a secret or two would also be wrought into the intricate mixture and layers of color and texture.

For me, a crazy quilt must have two distinctive features: random piecing and decorative embroidery. Only rarely were traditional quilting stitches used. Some crazy quilts were tied, but most were not. Often, the quilt had no batting. Crazy quilts were, and still are, art quilts, not utilitarian quilts. Crazy quilts are not made for warmth; they are made for their beauty and expressive qualities.

"It is extremely doubtful whether this class of needlework will ever lose its popularity. It serves so admirably to use odd bits of silk or other fabrics, and is really so artistic, if properly made, that its hold upon the feminine mind is not to be wondered at. It may interest many to know that the first 'crazy quilt' was made at the Tewksbury (Mass.) almshouse by a demented, but gentle, inmate, who delighted to sew together, in haphazard fashion, all the odd pieces given to her. One day a lady visitor was shown the quilt as a sample of 'poor Martha's crazy work.' The conglomeration of color, bright and dark, of every conceivable shape and size, caught the visitor's fancy, and within a week, she, herself, was making a crazy quilt. And thence the furore spread." So states the pamphlet, "Art Needlework," by Mme. Irene La Tour, c. 1916.

This is a lovely bit of myth. The "crazy" in crazy quilting had nothing to do with one's mental status. It referred, instead, to the random, or crazy, arrangement of fabric upon a foundation cloth and to the riot of color added through embroidery upon seams and within patches.

Some believe the random effect of piecing odd bits of cloth was a frugal effort continued from colonial times, when fabric was difficult to obtain in America. Every scrap of cloth would be saved and utilized into a "crumb" quilt. But, these working quilts were not adorned with seam treatments and embroidered motifs. They were strictly a means to join together scraps of cloth into a workable blanket.

A more widely held belief is that the Centennial Exposition of 1876 in Philadelphia, Pennsylvania, introduced Japanese aesthetics to Americans. The cracks, or crazing, on the Japanese ceramics resembled the crumb piecing of utilitarian quilts. The Japanese aesthetic of asymmetry and use of natural motifs and silk embroidery caught the imagination of American women. The two were then combined to produce stunning textile works of art known as crazy quilts.

The popularity of crazy quilting in the last quarter of the nineteenth century was widespread and intense. On March 16, 1885, a Crazy Work and Needle Art Show was held at the Horticultural Hall in Boston, Massachusetts. The show's catalogue listed 1,808 items on exhibit. It also included drawings for crazy-quilt stitches (1.3).

Some of the items listed within the catalogue include:

2. Crazy Quilt, consists of 5,000 pieces, exhibited by Miss Ella McArthur.

19. Pin Cushion of Crazy Work, made forty years ago, exhibited by Mrs. Roach.

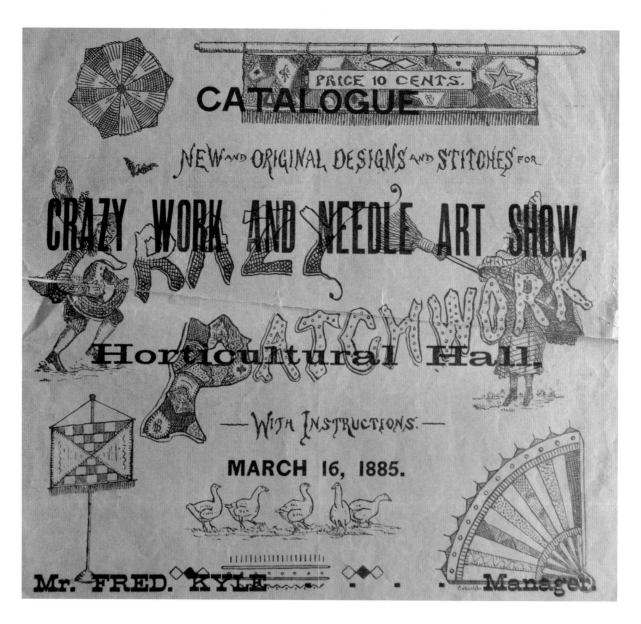

1.3

29. Sofa Pillow of Crazy Work, exhibited by Mrs. I. W. Derby, made by a gentleman, and contains 2,500 pieces.

42. Crazy Quilt, entered by Miss H. I. Ellis, made of pieces of the dresses of the leading society ladies in Washington.

123. Crazy Chair, upholstered by the exhibitor, Mrs. E. Dunne.

157. Crazy Dress, exhibited by Mrs. A. L. Tate.

174. Crazy Mantle Lambrequin, exhibited by Mrs. Geo. Pope.

189. Crazy Quilt, made by a lady sixty-four years of age, exhibited by Mrs. Thos. Cahill.

273. Crazy Fan, exhibited by Mrs. H. Hart.

274. Crazy Broom Case, exhibited by Mrs. H. L. Hart.

357. Crazy Quilt, seventy-three years of age, exhibited by Mrs. Lydia Beebe.

382. Crazy Quilt, made by a lady seventy-five years of age, thirty-five years ago, exhibited by Miss M. C. Stimpson.

398. Crazy Slumber Robe, exhibited by Mrs. Julie S. Warden.

421. Crazy Table Scarf, exhibited by Miss M. C. Belcher.

428. Crazy Sofa Pillow, containing one hundred and sixty pieces and fifty different stitches; exhibited by Miss Mabel L. Wilson, twelve years of age.

493. Crazy Table Scarf, exhibited by Miss Edith M. Bryant, age five years.

715. Crazy Quilt, exhibited by Mrs. F. Parker, made by a lady ninety-two years of age.

760. Crazy Quilt, made in eight days, exhibited by Mrs. J. L. Loveland.

776. Crazy Drapery, made by Mr. W. E. Prior.

792. Mat, made by Mrs. B. Knight, of Elkhart, Indiana, a lady eighty-six years of age, without glasses; exhibited by Mrs. D. W. Knight.

927b. Crazy Quilt, of 2,290 pieces, exhibited by Mrs. Wainwright. To be sold for $50.

973. Sofa Pillow, 3,276 pieces, exhibited by Mr. A. Cleveland; to be sold, $100. Would take $75.

1449. Satin Crazy Quilt, exhibited by Mrs. Ezra H. Crane.

1498. Crazy Tidy, exhibited by Mrs. J. D. Kidder.

1570. Quilt, exhibited by Mrs. H. R. Morse. This quilt contains 10,100 pieces.

1658a. Crazy Bible Cover, exhibited by Miss E. M. Garland.

1683. Embroidered Thermometer, exhibited by Mrs. William Cushing.

1794. Oriental Crazy Work, exhibited by Miss Sarah Smith.

1853. Crazy Quilt, exhibited by Miss A. Maud Smith. This was made when fourteen years of age, without a thimble.

It is interesting to note that in this 1885 exhibit, number 19 was a "Pin Cushion of Crazy Work," made forty years ago. That would mean it was made in 1845. I would like to see what the pincushion looked like! And number 382 was made thirty-five years before the exhibit, in 1850! Was it made as I define crazy quilting now, composed of random piecing and decorative embroidery? If so, that would date crazy quilting well before the 1876 centennial exhibition. I believe crazy quilting had been around for a number of years and simply acquired the name "crazy quilting" (crazy patch, crazy patchwork, or crazy work) after the exhibition, due to the resemblance of its mosaic-like patches to the crackled and crazed Japanese pottery glazes on display.

A quilter's age was often given if the maker was more than sixty years old or younger than fifteen years old. Apparently, to inquire of the age of a lady who fell between those parameters was impolite.

The exhibit also included entries made by men; I give several examples in the cited list. It seemed everyone wanted in on the fad of crazy quilting. Note that a sofa pillow, number 29, made by a gentleman, had 2,500 pieces. The size of the quilt isn't stated, but that is an ambitious project! However, Mrs. Morse's quilt, number 1570, contains 10,100 pieces. We have a winner!

Crazy quilts weren't the only crazy-style items entered into this exhibition. As the list shows, the exhibit included crazy bible covers, crazy drapery, crazy tidies, crazy broom covers, crazy pincushions, crazy chairs, crazy pillows, crazy clothing, and crazy table covers. Seemingly, anything made of fabric could be made in crazy-quilt fashion.

A few items have a price associated with them. A sofa pillow, made by Mr. Cleveland, containing 3,276 pieces was priced at $100. In today's dollars, that would equal $2,439. Mrs. Wainwright's crazy quilt, consisting of 2,290 pieces, was a bargain at $50, or $1,219.50 in today's dollars. Whether they sold or not is a mystery. Fred Kyle, the organizer of the Boston exhibit, offered gold and silver medals for the winners.

Figure 1.4 shows a detail of painted pansies on velvet on a Victorian crazy quilt.

In November 1885, another exhibition highlighted a dizzying display of crazy quilt work. This Crazy Patchwork and Needlework Show, held in Manhattan at the Masonic Temple on Twenty-third Street and Sixth Avenue, was also organized by Kyle. Hundreds of needlework examples were eagerly displayed, as each participant wanted to show off his or her skill with the needle. "An hour in the Masonic Hall will give anyone a fair idea of what women's work may come to when it becomes merely women's leisure employment," said the *New York Times*. The same article stated that one crazy table cover contained four million stitches! This cover was created by Mrs. C. Y. Bogert. I can't imagine the time it took to count those stitches, let alone to create them.

The lure of prizes of gold and silver medals (over eight hundred to be awarded) must have spurred the enthusiasm of the crazy quilters. There were prizes for the largest crazy quilt, the crazy quilt with the largest number of pieces, the greatest variety of stitches, the oddest design, the oddest materials, and the crazy quilt with the greatest number of distinguished autographs.

The State Historical Society of Missouri has, on display, a crazy quilt made by Mrs. David McWilliams. Her lovely velvet-bordered quilt is rather crazy as it contains a beautifully embroidered tree with, at the base of its trunk, two taxidermically stuffed chipmunks. I don't know if she entered her crazy quilt into either the Boston or Manhattan shows, but I would definitely have given her the prize for oddest materials!

Although prizes were offered for the Manhattan exhibition, none were ever awarded. The *New York Times*, on December 5, 1885, revealed that the Gorham Manufacturing Company, from whom Kyle had ordered the prize medals, was looking for his whereabouts. The newspaper reported that the announced awards "must have been a pleasant little fiction, invented as a gilded bait to lure on the owners of crazy quilts." So, the winners never received their prizes, but perhaps that was of little importance. As the *Times* commented snidely, the medals weren't even made of gold or silver, but "of base metal, silver plated, and worth only a few cents each—such medals, in fact, as no lady would care to possess."

This disappointment of fictitious prizes did not deter women and men from making crazy quilts. It seemed everyone either made a crazy-patch quilt or received one as a loving gift. And if they refrained from stitching a full-sized crazy quilt, then they made a crazy-worked "small," such as a table cover, wall pocket, or cushion.

The popularity of crazy quilting is illustrated in the following poem, published in *Good Housekeeping* magazine, October 25, 1890. It is one of several pieces on the new fad that appeared in a number of ladies' magazines.

The Crazy Quilt

Oh, say, can you see by the dawn's early light,
What you failed to perceive at the twilight's last gleaming;
A crazy concern that through the long night
O'er the bed where you slept was so saucily streaming;
The silk patches so fair,
Round, three-cornered, and square
Gives proof that the lunatic bed-quilt is there.
Oh, the crazy-quilt mania triumphantly raves,
And maid, wife, and widow are bound as its slaves
On that quilt dimly seen as you rouse from your sleep
Your long-missing necktie in silence reposes,
And the filoselle insects that over it creep,
A piece of your vest half-conceals, half discloses;
There is Kensington-stitch
In designs that are rich,
Snow-flake, arrasene, point russe, and all sich.
Oh, the crazy-quilt mania, how long will it rave?
And how long will fair woman be held its slave?
And where is the wife who so vauntingly swore
That nothing on earth her affections could smother?
She crept from your side at the chiming of four
And is down in the parlour at work on another.
Your breakfasts are spoiled,
And your dinners half-boiled,
And your efforts to get a square supper are foiled
By the crazy-quilt mania that fiendishly raves,
And to which all the women are absolute slaves.
And thus it has been since the panic began,

In many loved homes it has wrought desolation,
And cursed is the power by many a man,
That has brought him so close to the verge of starvation,
But make it she must,
She will do it or bust,
Beg, swap, and buy pieces or get them on trust,
Oh, the crazy-quilt mania, may it soon cease to rave
In the land of the free and the home of the brave.

—Unidentified

1.5

In July 1884, *Godey's Lady's Book* devoted several pages to crazy patch.
Godey's "Work Department" contained the following:

The design given for crazy patchwork, now so fashionable, shows
the different forms the pieces may be made, although a great deal
must be left to the ingenuity and taste of the person designing it.

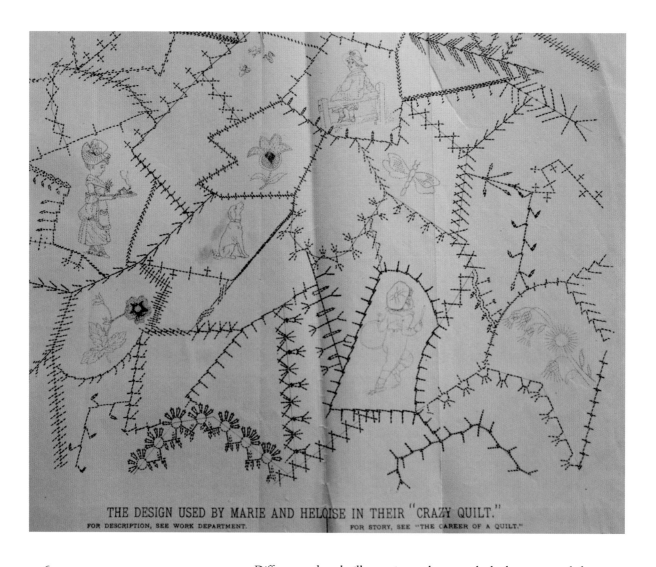

THE DESIGN USED BY MARIE AND HELOISE IN THEIR "CRAZY QUILT."
FOR DESCRIPTION, SEE WORK DEPARTMENT.   FOR STORY, SEE "THE CAREER OF A QUILT."

1.6

Different colored silks, satins, velvets, and plushes are used, harmony of color being aimed at in the arrangement. A piece of Canton flannel eighteen inches square is taken, and the pieces of silk arranged upon it. The edges of each piece should be turned in, and afterwards covered over with fancy stitches in colored silks or gold thread; numerous stitches are shown in our design; the greater the variety that adorn a quilt, the handsomer it is considered. The pieces are further ornamented with embroidered designs, or figures in etching, with colored silks. After the squares are completed, they are jointed together with fancy stitches, and the whole quilt should then have a border of plush nine inches deep put around it, with a lining throughout of satin. A pretty splasher can be made by reproducing the design to the size required, tracing it on coarse white linen, and doing the work with colored silks. It should then be trimmed all around with lace, and the two upper corners ornamented with ribbon bows.

Elsewhere in the same volume, a story, "The Career of a Crazy Quilt," was published. It tells of the correspondence between two friends, Marie (who resides in Albany, New York) and Heloise (who lives in Rochester, New York). Both women decide to create a crazy quilt (1.6). They exchange detailed letters—describing the project's conception, their gathering of materials, and the construction of their quilts. These letters give the readers a glimpse into one way a crazy quilt is made. They also include elements of soap opera.

It's amusing to see the "trials" the women face in garnering silks for their quilts. Marie's fiancée admonishes her not to be a boor and beg men for their silk handkerchiefs to include in her quilt. Heloise asks for samples from a dry-goods store and is handed bits of fabrics glued to cardboard, "because there were some ladies—he supposed they called themselves ladies—who were mean enough to come there for samples when they didn't want to buy anything at all, but just used the silks for patchwork; that the firm had been driven to this expedient in self-defence." And Marie writes that her "Papa was in a fearful rage this morning because I cut the lining out of his spring overcoat. I found it on the attic stairs and the sleeves were lined with lovely rose-colored striped satin, which I cut out."

What was it about crazy quilting that was so appealing to such a large number of the population of the United States? Seemingly no coat, hat, cravat, or dress was safe from the scissors of a woman who had caught crazy fever. (Nor were chipmunks!) Huge amounts of time and money were invested to create these personalized works of art.

Crazy quilting may have represented an accepted form of rebellion. The Victorian era did have a strict social and moral code. Rules to be followed unfailingly were everywhere. One certainly would not use one's dessert spoon to stir coffee. Nor would breakfast tea be served in the afternoon. How refreshing it must have been to color outside the lines with a crazy quilt! Although ideas and guidelines were suggested, they could be followed or ignored. And, if a person wanted to create a crazy quilt entirely with ideas gleaned from their own imagination, they were heartily encouraged.

At a time when women did not have the right to vote in the United States, she could still incorporate a political ribbon into her patchwork to

make her thoughts on the subject known. She could relay her individual reading preferences by embroidering phrases or titles of books or authors onto her crazy quilt. Her religious beliefs, or lack thereof, could be incorporated into her work by use of printed ribbons or embroidered symbols. Using the Victorian language of flowers, she could embroider a message known only to those who knew the code. Through her use of exquisite fabrics and silken threads, a woman could tell the world, "These are the things that are important to me; these are the things I love."

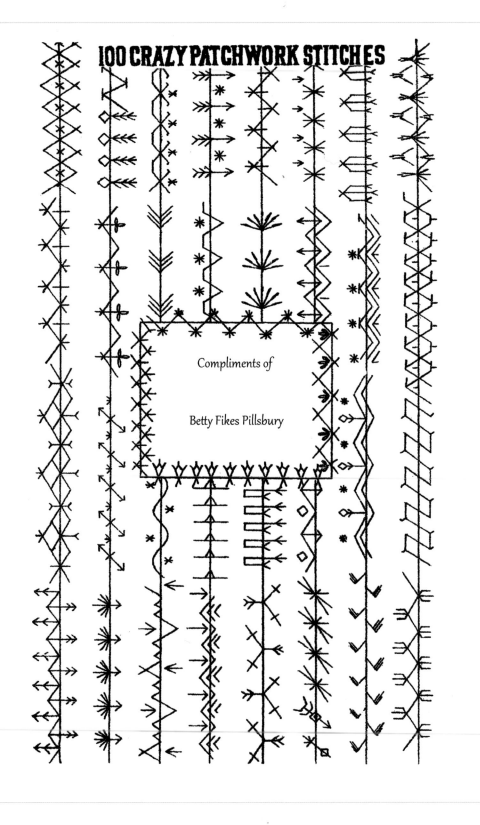

100 CRAZY PATCHWORK STITCHES

Compliments of

Betty Fikes Pillsbury

Personal Experience

how i go crazy

HOW DO I go crazy? Have three children under the age of five. Oops, sorry, I had a flashback for a moment. How do I crazy quilt? That's an entirely different question. And there is a method to my madness.

First, let me say that 95 percent of my work is done by hand. ALL the embroidery is done by hand and 95 percent of the piecing is also done by hand. I do put on long, straight borders by machine and will, occasionally, piece straight seams by machine. But, I enjoy handwork. I love the feel of fabric and thread in my hand. I enjoy the process of moving a needle through fabric and seeing the motif or seam treatment take shape. I delight in slow cloth. That's not to say that you can't do all your crazy quilting by machine. You certainly can. I prefer to do my work by hand, even with my rheumatoid arthritis, lupus, and osteoarthritis. I am very aware of ergonomics and am mindful not to stress my fingers and wrists overmuch. That's an important aspect of how I teach stitches—how to hold the fabric, needle, and thread in a manner that lessens the physical aggravation of hours at embroidery.

I taught myself to embroider when I was eight. I pestered my mother for floss, needles, and a stamped tea towel. Over the years, I have tried my hand at hedebo, or nué, pulled thread, drawn thread, goldwork, silk ribbon, beading, satin stitch, surface embroidery, cross stitch, stumpwork, blackwork, Mountmellick work, Richelieu embroidery, hardanger embroidery, shadow work, needle tatting, bobbin lace, crochet, quilting, needlepoint,

and sampler work, among others. I had to try anything and everything done with a needle—and some things done with hooks and bobbins! It is a passion that brings me great joy.

When I realized that crazy quilting could combine any and all these disparate needlework techniques into a beautiful, cohesive unit, the light came on for me. I'm sure there was an angelic choir singing as I made this discovery.

There are no rules in crazy quilting; do whatever pleases you. You may have heard that phrase if you have ever looked into making a crazy quilt. It is a nice idea. But, if you don't know how to start or what to do, how will you know how to do what pleases you? This book will provide you the tools to allow you to go crazy in a pleasing manner.

Crazy quilts are crazy because there is no discernible pattern. Crazy quilts also have decorative embroidery of some sort. Those are the only two requirements of a crazy quilt. If you have a quilt with no discernible pattern AND no embroidery, you have a scrap or crumb quilt. The side panels of Proud as A Peacock could be called a scrap quilt, if I had stopped with them (2.2a).

2.2*a*

But I didn't stop with just the piecing (2.2b). I embroidered, embellished, and elaborated until I went fully crazy!

My style of crazy quilting is not minimalist, nor is it so decorated that the fabric can no longer be seen. A minimalist quilt might be crazy-pieced with simple embroidery on the seams. I've seen other crazy quilts where the background isn't visible for all the embellishments. I'm probably just past center: my quilts are heavily embellished and embroidered,

2.2*b*

2.3a (left)
2.3b (right)

but the fabrics still play an integral part in the entire composition. A lot of time, thought, and money went into the placement of those fabrics! I want the fabrics, embroidery, and embellishments to exist joyfully with one another.

Style is definitely a matter of personal preference, as in any art. Some might enjoy Picasso while others sigh over Monet. Is one right or wrong? No. It all boils down to what you prefer. Take a look at crazy quilts and determine which style you prefer and wish to develop. Are you happy with straight lines and bold color? Do you lavish lace upon every surface? Does the phrase "too much bling" mean nothing to you? Is your preferred style organic with curvilinear lines and earthy colors? Crazy quilting can use any of these styles and more!

A pattern like Grandmother's Fan with embroidery is what I call almost crazy or an embellished quilt. This particular fan block has been hand embroidered and will be the center block of a fan-intense crazy quilt (2.3a). The rail-fence block (2.3b) is actually a showpiece for classes I teach, but you get the idea. Rail fence is a typical quilt pattern, one usually worked in cottons. I've stitched it here in taffetas and then embroidered on the seams and added motifs, thereby making it crazy. A "regular" quilt that follows a pattern and has no decorative stitching must, then, be sane.

You could have a quilt that seems to not know if it is crazy or not. It might have some portions that are pieced in a recognizable pattern and others that are truly crazy. In some antique crazy quilts, you can see a block of a sane quilt within a crazy-pieced panel. Alternating sane- and

crazy-quilt blocks can come together into one quilt (2.4). Borders of a sane quilt can be crazy quilted. Or the centers can be crazy quilted with a sane-block surround.

Call it what you will, but I consider a quilt crazy if a significant portion is crazy patched and embroidered. Crazy Diamonds, which was inspired by an antique quilt, is of that sort (2.5). It is arranged not in blocks, but in diamond shapes. Some of the diamonds feature an embroidered motif; alternating diamonds are fully crazy patched and embroidered. Every

stitch of this quilt is done by hand, from piecing to embroidery, to sashing, to binding. Yeah, that's crazy.

Crazy quilts traditionally have been pieced with fancy fabrics like velvet, satin, taffeta, damask, and ribbons. However, you could make a crazy quilt that is completely pieced of cotton fabrics. Proud as A Peacock is made with cotton fabrics only—LOTS of embellishments, but only cotton fabrics. Most often, I use a blend of fabrics. Because my crazy-quilted projects are for show, I can blend different fabric contents without worrying about washing. I do not pre-wash new fabrics. Usually, a quilter pre-washes a quilt's fabrics so they don't shrink when the completed quilt is washed. I'm not going to wash my art, so I don't have to worry about that. If I cut up an old blouse, dress, or curtain, then I wash that fabric to get out any soil or smell. I enjoy working with cotton batiks and the beautifully printed quilting cottons available today. Elderberry Fairy has a printed cotton with the Elderberry Fairy on it. The original artwork is by Cicely Mary Barker on a fabric printed by Michael Miller Fabrics. Lovely cottons combined with luscious taffeta, elegant brocade, sumptuous velvet, and slinky silk dupioni can create stunning results in crazy quilting.

Another important aspect of my crazy quilts is the layering—visual layering. I start with the initial layer of fabrics. I add a layer of trims, laces, sew-ons, et cetera. Then comes a layer of embroidery. Perhaps there is another layer of buttons, charms, and beads. Sometimes the layers have layers. I may place layers of embroidery on one another or embroidery on a sew-on trim. Layering can help bring the eye around the composition of the project by introducing color and shapes. Layering gives interest and depth and draws the viewer into your art. It's rather like a mixed-media collage done with needle and thread.

The crazy quilts I make are not utility quilts. They aren't made for warmth or to snuggle under. They are made simply for beauty's sake, to be spread artistically on a bed (and then moved away before sleep so the delicate embellishments aren't ruined), hung on a wall, or made into a pillow, pincushion, journal cover, handbag, et cetera. Whatever can be made of fabric can be crazy quilted. I've made lampshades, trinket boxes, angel Christmas tree toppers, ornaments, bracelets, clothing, tablecloths, runners—I think you get the idea. Crazy quilts are made to be admired. They are like any other piece of art that is displayed. However, if you plan to use your crazy quilt as a utility quilt, ensure that all the fabrics, embroideries, and embellishments are washable, dryable, and durable!

Traditionally, crazy quilts were not quilted. Occasionally, you will see an antique crazy quilt that has been tied. Usually, though, they had neither quilting stitches nor tying. A utility quilt with batting inserted for warmth needed quilting stitches or tying through all its layers in order to hold the batting in place. Some of my crazy quilts have quilting stitches. More often than not, the quilting stitches were added so the crazy quilt could be entered into a quilt show that required such stitching. Sometimes I do add quilting as a visual part of the piece. I tie some of my crazy quilts. Sometimes, tying is done to stabilize a heavily embellished front that may sag under the weight of those embellishments when it is hung upon a wall. Sometimes, tying is a requirement of a quilt show. If the crazy quilts are small, I may neither tie nor quilt the piece. What I do tomorrow may be a different story.

There are several ways in which a crazy quilt can be constructed. In the quilt Proud as A Peacock, the central panel isn't even crazy quilted; it is appliquéd with embellishments. The side panels have been crazy quilted. Each panel has been constructed as a large piece. Those side pieces were added to the central panel, which does have machine quilting on it. This piece was made for a contest that insisted that only the sponsor's line of cotton fabrics be used. I completed the piece in time, but forgot to send its picture in by the deadline. My kingdom for a better memory!

A crazy quilt can be "whole cloth." That's when the entire crazy quilt is one large "block." Perchance shows how the entire crazy-quilted portion was worked as one large piece (2.6). Borders were added after the crazy-quilted section was pieced and embellished. Some of its larger embroidery pieces, such as the fairies, were hand embroidered on fabric, then added as any other fabric would be (2.7a). The fairy outlines came from Dover Publications books. The fairy queen has hand painting, satin stitching with silk and rayon threads, and metallic highlights (2.7b). The smaller fairy has hair of bullion knots, a face worked in split stitch, and satin-stitched wings highlighted with metallic threads (2.7c).

Included in Perchance is a rebus, a patch with embroidered plants related to fairy lore, and a secret message in a spider's web à la *Charlotte's Web*. The quilt has a three-dimensional book that opens to reveal a quotation, a stumpwork thistle, and satin-stitched flowers that garnered a national judge's praise stating "your machine embroidery is outstanding." Uh, all that embroidery is by HAND, but thanks.

2.6

2.7a

2.7b

2.7c

2.8

2.9a (left)
2.9b (right)

A crazy quilt can be made of blocks that are then sewn together. Homage to Ardelia (2.8) has a center block that is a hand-embroidered monogram (2.9a). It is centered and appliquéd onto a larger block that has been pieced as one whole (2.9b). The quilt has a velvet burgundy border with gold metallic hand stitching. Surrounding that are alternating crazy and sane blocks, with no sashing between them. I then placed another burgundy border, this time in cotton and studded with beads. An ice cream border surrounds the entire quilt. I placed beads on the burgundy cotton border and elsewhere throughout the quilt to hide the stitches that tie the quilt together.

My great-grandmother, Ardelia Benson, who died before I was born, was a quilt maker and herbalist. I know where I got a significant portion of my genetic material! When working on this quilt, I imagined if she and I had collaborated on a quilt, what the effect would be. I used antique and modern materials and motifs, hopefully crafted into a cohesive whole. This quilt won many awards. The borders were added by machine; everything else is by hand.

I hand embroidered the monogram, then placed it in the central portion of the quilt. The "B" was stitched in a single strand of silk thread. A metallic thread was used to stem stitch around the letters. A few beads were added for highlights. Previously, I had taught near San Francisco. During an enjoyable shopping trip to La Ribbonerie, I purchased a length of spider-and-web ribbon, not knowing what use I would have for it, because I was amused by it. Fast forward a few years later to when I was working on Homage to Ardelia. I put the monogram in the center of the quilt, remembered the ribbon, and had—just—enough for the surround.

I used gold embroidery on the velvet strips surrounding the center portion. You can see the pattern drawn on the tissue paper and basted in place (2.10a). It was stem stitched by hand. Some outer blocks were completed and, in figure 2.10b, are being auditioned for placement.

Figure 2.11a shows one of the blocks. The beads in the corner provided a way to tie the quilt without the ties showing. I tied with a pearl cotton: bringing up the pearl cotton on the back, going through the disc bead on the front, going down through to the backing, then tying the ends off.

The inspiration for this block came from an antique crazy quilt in an exhibit. The maker had stitched a small circle composed of tiny bits of fabric. I wanted to take it a step further by having a circular border of silk ribbon forget-me-nots. I felt it still needed something, so I made the beaded picot lace for an outer border.

Figure 2.11b shows the ice-cream-cone border being auditioned. Often, I will pin up work temporarily to see if the arrangement works. I'll leave it up for a time and walk quickly by to see if something glaring jumps out at me, or to see if there is a color or a motif that needs balancing. I could see that another burgundy border was needed to separate the crazy-quilted blocks from the border. I added that in a cotton fabric and used beads to tie that as well.

Sometimes, the blocks aren't square, but are diamond-shaped.

Crazy Diamonds was made completely by hand: the piecing, embroidery, sashing, and binding (2.5). I made it in response to the American Quilter's Society 2009 Knoxville Quilt Expo contest, Great Embroidered Quilts. Immediately, I thought a crazy quilt was the perfect vehicle. (I always think that.) Inspired by an antique crazy quilt made of diamond blocks, I set about making my own version. I wanted a large center diamond surrounded by alternating crazy-pieced diamonds and diamonds that featured an embroidered motif. The deadline was early April of 2009. I made a plan and worked diligently to meet that deadline.

As a few months went by, I realized what a monumental task I had set before myself to complete in a short time! The deadline was rapidly approaching and there was still a LOT to do. However, I felt if I really focused and let the housework go by the wayside (not a hardship), I could actually complete this in time! Then, my daughter called to tell me she was going into labor—earlier than we expected. Frantically, I pulled the uncompleted diamonds together, threw in the threads and silk ribbons and beads I thought I might need and drove to her house. This was her first baby. What a joyous time! I knelt down in front of my daughter, her belly bulging, and whispered to the baby: "Please, little one, Granny needs just a little more time to meet this deadline and you aren't really due for a few more weeks. Can you wait just a few more days so I can get this quilt done?" My daughter was not pleased with this conversation. Especially since Raffaele listened! Marathon stitching ensued, and the quilt was completed, photographed, and sent by the deadline. Then, the baby was born.

Crazy Diamonds won first place in the contest. It went on to win many more awards, including first place at the Vermont Quilt Festival (with a special ribbon for handwork), the Empire QuiltFest, and the Bennington QuiltFest. It also won ribbons at the Road to California Quilt Show and the (Hershey, Pennsylvania) Quilt Odyssey, as well as a few vendor's choice and people's choice awards.

Because the diamonds were such a difficult shape with which to work, I went about setting up this quilt's layout somewhat differently. Instead of sewing the diamonds together, as they would be treated in a sane quilt, I drafted the diamonds and sashing area on a large interfacing (2.12). The diamonds were then basted into their proper place. The large center diamond features a brown velvet background with a floral arrangement of roses, daisies, and forget-me-nots. The roses were made out of satin fabric. The other flowers are made of silk-ribbon embroidery.

The leaves are silk-chenille embroidery. I dyed the lace hummingbird and butterfly (2.13).

The diamond blocks are butted against one another. The velvet-ribbon sashing was then sewn down over the abutment. I then sewed diamond-shaped beads at the sashing intersections (2.14). I did this after I attached the backing. Using a pearl cotton, I tied the quilt while sewing

the buttons on. I started the pearl cotton on the back of the quilt, came through the bead on the front, went back through the backing, then tied off. Each bead was done in this manner. This held the quilt together so it could be hung on a wall without sagging.

Borders can be crazy quilted. The central portion of Roses and Paisleys is embroidered with the addition of wired-ribbon flowers that I made (2.15). Beadwork and a few purchased butterfly motifs were added.

Crazy-quilt borders on two sides provide an asymmetric balance to the piece. Rose and paisley motifs were embroidered throughout the piece.

The borders on the top and left side are made from a velvet ribbon and a light pink, wired ribbon that has been gathered and stitched with an antique blanket stitch in gold metallic thread. A student sent me a picture of an antique crazy quilt that had a ribbon edge done in this fashion. I adapted the idea slightly, then added the velvet ribbon.

The shape of the "quilt" can be an odd shape, like this fan crazy quilt (2.16).

Or, it can be a heart shape (2.17).

2.16

2.17

Beginning Your Crazy Quilt

Making a Foundation and Choosing Fabrics

RAZY QUILTING is pieced on a muslin foundation. Because the scrap pieces of fabric you are using may be cut on the bias or curved, the foundation provides a stability that keeps the entire quilt from moving around and becoming cattywampus. When you sew pieces together, you also sew through the muslin foundation. This stabilizes everything. Always use a ¼" seam and press each seam as you go along. Trim any excess fabric in the seams.

To make a foundation, let's start one section at a time with a block. A 9" finished block is a good size. You can make just one and finish it as a pillow, make many and make a wall hanging, or make LOTS and make a quilt.

Start by drawing a 9½" block onto a 12" square of muslin (3.1). The 9½" measurement gives a finished block of 9" plus ¼" seam allowance on all four sides. I use a quilter's ruler that measures 9½", as this makes precise measuring very easy. Then, flip the muslin over and trace the square on the back. You will need this line on the back toward the end, trust me. Some people like the extra muslin all around their block as it gives them something to hold onto as they do embroidery. Some people like to cut the muslin to exactly 9½" for a 9" finished block. Experiment and see what you like. I tend to switch back and forth.

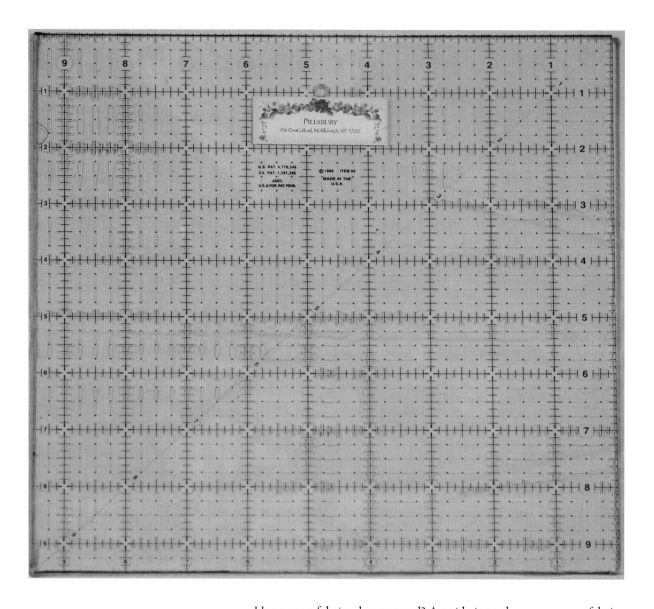

3.1

How many fabrics do you need? A guide is to choose as many fabrics as inches in the measurement of your block. A 9" square might use nine fabrics, more or less. A 12" block might have twelve patches, more or less. This is just a guide; as you become more proficient, use your own judgment. I find this is the way I piece most often because it gives me patches of fabric large enough for embroidered motifs and enough room for interesting seam treatments. You could artfully piece a 9" block using six fabrics or twenty fabrics! But, let's try nine patches of fabric to begin. You can also repeat fabrics within a block, perhaps using a focus fabric several times, still ending with nine patches.

If you have difficulty choosing fabrics, start with a focus fabric. Find a print fabric which appeals to you (floral, geometric, scenic). Coordinate the other fabrics with the colors of the focus fabric. Then, you can opt not to use the focus fabric, as the other fabrics will coordinate beautifully. Or, choose fabrics at random. Go for a variety of values (lights and darks), textures (smooth and rough), and scale (size of the prints). You could also opt to go monochromatic (various shades of one color) or monofabric (all satins or all velvets, for example).

It's okay to put a pattern against another pattern and a solid against another solid. However, maintain an overall balance to your work by your distribution of pattern and color. Also remember that when two very busy prints are side by side, the seam treatment becomes more difficult to see.

I mix silks, cottons, rayons, and blends within one piece. Use new and used fabrics. Scour thrift stores for prom dresses, neckties, and other interesting garments. Look in the drapery department of fabric stores for unusual pieces.

Working with velvet can be tricky as the fabric's nap makes the velvet creep and crawl around! You can fuse a lightweight interfacing to the back side of a velvet to prevent that creeping. An interfacing also works well with slinky, lightweight silks, giving them a little more hand for stability and shadowing.

In figure 3.2, the solid blue fabric I chose might seem, at first, to overwhelm the colors of the other fabrics a bit. However, there is blue in the print fabric. You must also consider that embellishment layers will be

added. When embellishing, you can incorporate more color to even out the patchwork colors.

Piecing Your Crazy Quilt Block

I have developed the "fifty-two-card-pick-up" method for crazy quilting. Do you remember this game from childhood? An older sibling would ask you to play a card game, fifty-two-card-pick-up. Upon brandishing the cards, he would let the cards fly from his hands and say, "There are fifty-two cards; pick them up." This is amusing to the older sibling, but not so much for the younger.

However, this game creates an effect very like the pattern of a crazy quilt. Imagine pieces of fabric falling from above and landing in a haphazard fashion. Some fabrics would line up side by side, some would overlap another (what I call a nook and cranny) and some would fan out. This is how a crazy quilt is pieced. There are straight seams, nooks and crannies, and curves. In figure 3.3a, Birds of a Feather (3.4) has been pieced, but no embellishments have been placed yet, except for the hand-stitched peacock in the center, which was embroidered and appliquéd in as one of the patches (3.3b). Note the straight seams, the curves, and the nooks and crannies (patches that jut out onto other patches).

Choose any two fabrics to begin. The first seam will be a simple straight seam. Place the fabrics so they are slightly off-center. Also, ensure

3.5

the first seam does not run parallel to any of the square's edges. If the first seam parallels the block's edge, it can become difficult to get out of the habit of matching straight edges and the block may end up looking like a log cabin block on drugs!

Place the two fabrics, right sides together, on the muslin. Use a single strand of sewing thread in the needle to stitch a running stitch ¼" in from the edge. Remember to stitch through the muslin too! Press the seam. Open the fabric and press the seam again. This is called sew and flip (3.5).

Now let's add a curve. Cut a curved shape in the next piece of fabric you want to use. You can use a cardboard template or simply cut a random curve. I just cut random curves. Press under a ¼" seam allowance along the curve to the back of the fabric. Lay the curve onto the two pieces that have been sewn down. I like to audition where the fabrics will go. To do this, move the curve around until it looks pleasing. Pin the curved fabric in place and appliqué where it overlaps a fancy fabric, sewing the curved piece only at the place where the two fabrics meet. Do not sew just to the muslin background. When you have completed sewing, trim the excess fabric to ¼" from under that appliquéd seam (3.6).

3.6

DON'T APPLIQUÉ HERE.

To appliqué, use a very fine needle. I like a quilting #10 or a between #10. Use one

strand of sewing thread; tie a knot in the end of the thread. Keep the patch that is being appliquéd on your left. Come up as close to the folded edge of the appliquéd piece as you can. Using a finer needle will allow you to get quite close to the edge. With the tip of your needle, "fall off the edge of the fold" right at the level where the thread originally came up, and plunge the needle tip down through the fabric below (in figure 3.7, the mauve silk on the right). When you plunge down, you will go through the fancy fabric AND the muslin below. Remember, crazy quilting is done on the muslin foundation. Stitching through all layers secures everything from shifting.

Once the tip of the needle is plunged down, you will come back up (through all layers) to emerge about ¼" away on the fold of the appliquéd piece. This is done in one smooth motion. Well, it will get smooth with practice. Don't stab the needle all the way through the fabric and try to stab back up. You will have better control and, therefore, hidden stitches if you use the scooping motion.

Once you have emerged, draw the needle and thread completely through. Now you are ready to appliqué the next stitch, again with the tip of the needle falling off the edge of the fold. Once you have stitched the appliquéd patch in place, remembering to only appliqué where two fancy fabrics meet, not where there is only one fancy fabric and muslin, you can lift up the appliquéd fabric and trim away extra fabric from the seam allowance (3.8).

Next, add a nook and cranny. Audition a piece of fabric onto the curved piece. When you are happy with the placement, turn under the

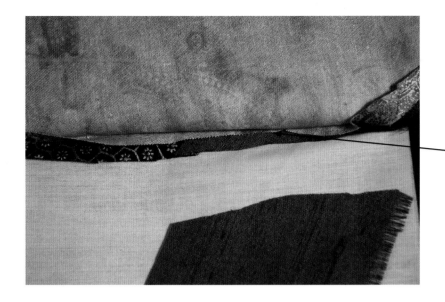

3.8

EXCESS FABRIC HAS BEEN
CUT AWAY FROM THE SEAM.

short edge by ¼". Now, sew and flip the long edge. When you finish that, you will go back and appliqué the short, turned-under edge.

Continue with straight seams, curves, and nooks and crannies until the block is pieced. You don't have to go in that order (straight, curve, nook); do whatever appeals to you. This provides an organic, free-flowing look that lends itself to delightful embellishment.

If you work from the inside to the outside with just straight seams, you often end up with choppy, inelegant pieces that look awkward, as if you painted yourself into a corner and couldn't figure a way out. With my method, you can't work yourself into a corner, because you can simply

3.9

THIS LONG EDGE IS SEWN
AND FLIPPED. MAKE SURE
TO TURN UNDER THAT
SHORT EDGE FIRST!

THIS SHORT EDGE IS TURNED
UNDER ¼" AND APPLIQUÉD
AFTER THE LONG EDGE
IS SEWN.

43

appliqué a piece at the edge or add a straight seam or curve. Because you will have been varying the styles of your seams and stitches all along, a different style won't seem out of place when it is used at the edges, as might be the case if you were forced to change your style of stitching there. Your work will flow more artistically.

Continue with the piecing. In the lower right corner of figure 3.10, a straight edge has been sewn and flipped. A concave curve has been appliquéd with a light brown moire fabric in the upper left. I chose the moire to frame the flowers in the printed cotton in the central portion of the block. Notice that there are two raw edges. Oh no!! How do I get around this? Adding a nook and cranny or a curve!

See? All our problems have been solved and the block looks very organic (3.11). To cover the bottom of that light brown moire, a mauve fabric has been placed as a nook and cranny. Then, a mustard silk was appliquéd on with a curved seam. The flocked black fabric was then added with the straight seam sewn and flipped and the curve appliquéd down. Follow this technique and there'll be no painting yourself into a

corner. I've put all the pitfalls you might run into when creating a quilt in this one block; all the pitfalls have been handled successfully.

When you are done piecing, turn the block over so the muslin is facing up. Remember that drawn outline of your square? Now it will come

3.12

into use. Either hand or machine stitch along that drawn line, through all the layers of fabric (3.12). This stabilizes the edges and helps your block stay square during embellishment. You can trim the excess fabric now or wait until later.

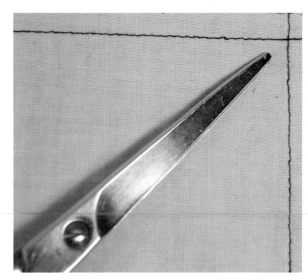

Now the embellishment, which includes the embroidery, laces, beadwork, and other enhancements, can begin. Figure 3.13 shows the block in progress. Antique lace meanders across seam lines and a photo transfer of a cigarette silk has been added. A wired ribbon has been scrunched around the silk, forming a frame. A blue silk thread has been used for chevron stitching along a seam.

In figure 3.14, the block has had more embroidery and embellishments added. Around the framed cigarette silk, I've added silk ribbon roses and leaves and pearls. The flowers just to the right of the cigarette silk are made with a silk bias ribbon. Chain stitch, straight stitches, and beads have been added. A tied herringbone stitch is on the seam next to it. I sewed crystals along the bottom of that seam. A heart bead with a stem-stitched scroll was placed on the light brown moire patch. On the mustard silk I have added a hand-dyed lace butterfly. Notice how it picks up the blue from the patch at the bottom. Featherstitch in a free-form pattern forms the bush on which the butterfly alights. Blanket stitch in pink silk is on the concave portion of the light brown moire. There are wee, tiny French knots in green at the end of the "fingers." With the printed fabric, I have highlighted the shapes by stem stitching in a gold metallic thread. On the mauve dupioni silk on the right, I stitched a paisley with a bullion rose. The seam is a series of straight stitches, which form boxes. More straight stitches and beads were added. On the left side of that seam, I added bugle beads and seed beads to form triangles. Along the curve of the pink and gold fabric is a seam of shadow chevron stitches with French knots added at the platform. Cretan stitches with lazy dai-

sies and crystals form the seam below the cigarette silk. The spiderweb
was stitched with a #40 weight Madeira metallic made for machines, but
sewn by hand! Featherstitch in a gold-colored silk lines the blue patch.
Within the blue patch is a bouquet of flowers done in cast-on stitch with
leaves of lazy daisies. A bow of silk ribbon meanders throughout the blue
patch. At the bottom right, a chenille motif has been stitched across four
patches. Remember, you don't have to stay on the lines.

BEGINNING YOUR CRAZY QUILT

An Alternative to Sewing Blocks Together

Sometimes, I want to make just one block and have it be the center of attention. Often with crazy quilting, there is a problem with turning under seams and not having a smooth edge because crazy quilting uses so many different weights of fabrics within one piece. Here I have made a crazy quilt block that isn't square, but is in a heart shape (3.15). Instead of tracing a square onto the muslin, I drew a heart. Then, I pieced as I would if the block were a square. See the straight seams, curves, and nooks and crannies? The running stitch on the heart shape holds all the fabrics in place and helps prevent skewing of the fabrics while you embellish. The heart is embellished and ready to be applied to a background fabric.

The next step is to trim the excess fabric to ¼" of the running-stitch outline of the heart. Be quite careful as you do this. Often, I will apply Fray Check to the cut edges to prevent raveling. Just a small line of this liquid will halt raveling. Let the Fray Check dry before proceeding.

Then, I chose a pretty background fabric on which to place the heart. I chose an ivory damask to coordinate with the ivory embellishments of the pink heart (3.16). After placing the heart in the center of the back-

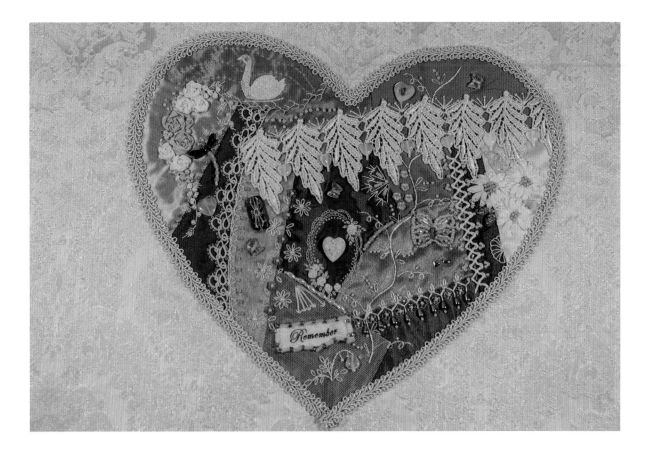

ground fabric, I used a single strand of sewing thread and tacked the heart in place. Now I won't have a lumpy, bumpy, turned-under edge to spoil the look of my work.

This, of course, left a raw edge of the heart showing. To remedy that, I sewed a gimp edging over the cut edge. Choose a gimp wide enough and dense enough to cover the raw edges. A lace would not work because the raw edges would show through. Too narrow a gimp would make it difficult to hide those edges.

Figure 3.17 shows cigarette silks from my collection. You have my permission to copy them onto fabric for use in your own work. You may not sell these silks nor copy them for another use. Purchase specialty-fabric sheets that can run through your computer printer. Scan these images into your computer and print them onto fabric, following the manufacturer's directions.

3.16

PANSIES

MAB QUEEN OF IRELAND, 15TH CENTURY

ZIRA CIGARETTES

UNITED STATES
OF AMERICA

Preparing for Embroidery

The first question I ask myself is "what do I want embroidered and where?" If I chose a particular theme for my crazy-quilt piece, be it a block, a jacket, or an entire quilt, do I want certain motifs that will reflect that theme? Of course! Sometimes, I will know exactly what motif I would like to incorporate before I even start a project. If that is the case, I may embroider that motif onto a piece of fancy fabric, then set it aside and use it like a patch of any other fancy fabric that I piece into my crazy quilt. I may consider the embroidery a major component of the crazy quilt and appliqué it into a central portion after the piecing has been completed.

Sometimes, I don't know what I want to embroider until after the entire project is pieced and I hear a certain fabric say, "Wouldn't that little fairy motif look spectacular in this space?" Sometimes, I may have embroidered lots of seams and other motifs, only to find an area on the quilt that looks sparse. (Heaven forbid!) I will then go looking for a motif that will fill that area.

Often, I will look for a motif that will repeat a shape or color to enhance the overall composition of a quilt. That motif might be placed in the center of a patch or it might straddle two or more patches. The motif might become a seam treatment through repetition.

Materials

Needles. Purchase quality needles. Cheaper needles might have burrs, which make embroidery difficult because threads will catch on the needle; dull points, which make getting through fabric difficult; and inconsistent sizes, which frustrate the embroiderer. They also tend to be weak and may break quickly. Spend the few extra dollars to get good needles in a variety of sizes. The size you need depends on the thread you use: the higher the number, the finer the needle. A size 10 is a finer needle than a size 4.

I don't get too caught up in the exact size of a needle. Use the finest needle that you can comfortably thread with the type of thread you are using. The finer needle will leave a smaller hole in your fabric.

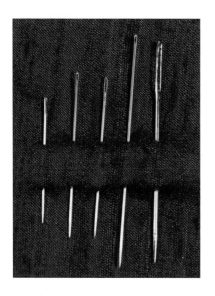

3.18

Types of Needles:

Betweens have short shanks and sharp tips; these are good for quilting stitches.

Sharps have a sharp tip (!) and a larger eye than a regular sewing needle; these are good for general embroidery.

Crewels have a sharp tip and elongated eye. The eye is easier to thread when using several plies of floss or when using various thicker threads. This is the needle I use the most.

Milliners (Straw) has a shaft and an eye that are the same diameter. This is the perfect needle for creating bullion knots, which involves wrapping the thread around the needle many times and pulling it through. Because the eye of the needle does not flare out, the wraps slide off easily.

Chenille is a large needle with a large eye and sharp point. This is used for ribbon embroidery and for handling larger needlepoint threads.

Hoops. Generally, I do not use a hoop for embroidery. I taught myself to embroider without one and can manage the tension of the fabric and threads without one. However, if I am doing a complex satin-stitch motif, I may use a hoop. Use one if you are comfortable with it!! Use whatever gets the job done in a manner that you enjoy. Experiment with a wooden hoop, a plastic hoop, q-snap frames, and needlework frames. Find what works best for you.

Foundation. Crazy quilting is done with a muslin foundation. I like to get a muslin that is very easy to needle through. The muslin acts as a stabilizer so the fancy fabrics, which may be cut on the bias, don't shift. If your embroidery is done before it will be pieced into the crazy quilt, decide whether the fabric needs a foundation for the embroidery. If the fabric is very thin or slippery, it will benefit from a muslin foundation or an iron-on, lightweight stabilizer.

Fabrics. Because my work will not be washed, I don't concern myself about the fiber content of the fabrics that I choose for crazy quilting. I am interested in color and texture. I might recycle a silk blouse, a prom dress, or a wedding gown. I buy new fabrics of various sorts. I look in home-decorating sections of fabric stores. I haunt quilt shops for printed cottons. I check out bridal shops and ask for their discarded scraps. Out-of-fashion ties that are no longer worn become treasured bits of silk worked into a quilt. An inherited handkerchief that has grown threadbare may still offer portions that are usable and beautiful in your project.

Embroidering on velvet can be especially tricky. Not only can it slip and slide while being pieced (use an iron-on stabilizer), it can be difficult to mark for embroidery. You can put the pattern on the backside of the

velvet by using an iron-on transfer, freehand drawing, or basting tissue paper onto which a pattern has been drawn. Velveteen has a lower nap and is easier to piece and embroider.

Threads. I admit it, I am a thread junkie. I LOVE embroidery threads. I use cottons, silks, rayons, wools, acrylics, and metallics, among others. I love thick threads, thin threads, shiny threads, matte threads, couching threads, variegated threads, overdyed threads, et cetera. Needlepoint shops have lovely threads to explore. The resources section in this book lists some online sources. For me, the most interesting crazy quilts use an eclectic mix of fabrics and threads. The interplay of all the elements delights the eye. You can make an interesting crazy quilt by using just one stitch in a variety of embroidery threads. Think of featherstitch done in #8 pearl cotton, DMC cotton floss, Wildflowers, Madeira metallic #40 weight, Frosty Rays, Watercolors, #8 Kreinik metallic braid, 4 mm silk ribbon, silk buttonhole twist, chenille, rayon floss, Splendor silk floss, Empress flat silk floss, and/or sewing thread (3.19).

Cotton floss is an embroiderer's base in stock. Everyone should have cotton floss in their needlework bag. Found in nearly every store that sells fabrics, needlework supplies, or crafts, cotton floss is an American staple.

Transferring Designs

Iron-on transfers. These are suitable for many light-colored, smooth fabrics and can be used on some light-colored, textured fabrics. Experimentation is needed to see what is suitable. Usually, iron-on transfers markings do NOT wash out. Ensure embroidery covers all lines.

Tissue Paper. Any design can be traced onto tissue paper. Tissue paper with the drawn design is basted in place on fabric. The design is embroidered through the tissue paper and fabric, then the tissue paper is torn away when the embroidery is complete. It can be very tedious to remove all the tissue paper, so generally, I only stem stitch through the tissue paper. I then remove the tissue paper, and complete the embroidery.

Saral Transfer Paper. This is a waxless "carbon" paper that comes in light and dark colors. Place Saral paper on top of your fabric, then place the pattern of choice on top of the Saral. Use a fine-line mechanical pen to trace over the lines of the design. The image will transfer to the fabric. Any marks will brush off after the embroidery is finished. Sometimes, however, the lines will disappear before the embroidery can be completed.

Water-Soluble Material. A design is traced onto the water-soluble material and then basted onto fabric. The design is embroidered through the soluble material and fabric. When the embroidery is completed, dunk the piece in water and the water-soluble material "melts" away. Make sure the fabric on which you embroider is able to be submersed in water.

Marking Pens. Many varieties are available on the market place today. I highly recommend following the manufacturer's directions and TESTING the pen on your fabric first! Some air-soluble pens are not always air soluble. Others are so air soluble that the marks may disappear before embroidery is completed. Water-soluble-pen marks may show up in a few months as faint yellow marks. Some water-soluble pens may not erase at all.

Pigma Pens and Zig Pens. These are archival quality, fine-line markers used directly on fabric. The line is so fine that embroidery can be done directly on the marks and they usually do not show. Nice if you can draw a motif freehand, or if you want to embroider over handwriting.

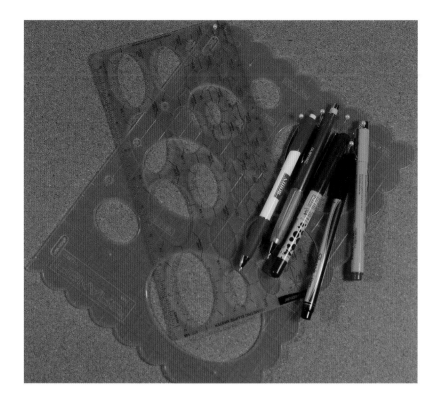

Tiger Tape. This temporary striped adhesive tape is used by quilters to measure out quilting stitches. Once the stitching is done, the tape is removed, and no adhesive remains. I like to use tiger tape for spacing out herringbone and chevron stitches.

Templates. These can be made from various materials, including heavy cardstock and plastics. They are useful for placement of some seam treatments.

Stencils. Stencils are made from various materials, usually plastic. They are useful for motifs. Look for drafting circles and similar templates in an art store. Other templates and stencils can be found in the scrapbooking section of craft stores.

Slips. These were used in medieval embroidery. A motif was embroidered onto a piece of fabric, sometimes using counted-thread technique, sometimes using surface embroidery. After the motif was embroidered, it was cut out and then appliquéd to the main textile. In this case, a motif might be embroidered onto a small fancy fabric and then cut out and applied to a crazy-quilt block.

I do not recommend using a graphite pencil or ballpoint pen to mark directly onto fabric. Each generally ends up smearing; that smear becomes a permanent part of the fabric!

Dover Publications is a vast source of line drawings suitable for use in crazy quilting. Their themed-motif books include everything from fairies to Art Deco motifs to monograms. I highly recommend perusing their site. Look to coloring books for more motif ideas. I have an extensive collection of Victorian books with ideas for crazy quilting. I also have a large collection of antique crazy quilts. I spend much time poring over motifs and seam treatments for inspiration. An Internet search or time at your local library will also provide tons of ideas for use in crazy quilting.

Look for alternative sources of inspiration. A walk through your neighborhood may present a wrought-iron-fence pattern that could become a seam treatment. A stroll through the woods may inspire a leaf-embroidery motif. Perhaps your favorite television series will motivate you to stitch a Celtic knot, stone circle, wolf, abbey, or zombie!

Starting Your Embroidery Thread

If you are working with cotton floss, the thread must be stripped first. Cotton floss comes in skeins and is bound by two bands: one end has a wider band, the other end has a narrower band. Cotton floss has six plies, meaning that there are six individual strands of thread making up the larger thread of the skein. To use the thread, you must separate the larger thread into plies.

First, let's get the thread out of the skein without swearing! I see many people grasp a loose end and pull on the thread and wind up with a knot. There's a secret to knot-free cotton floss! Begin by grasping the wider band around the floss, gripping it between your left hand's index finger and thumb. Wrap your pinkie finger around the narrow band (3.21a).

Gently pull on the cut end of floss; you should be able to slowly pull on that thread and not have a tangled mess.

Then, you will need to separate the plies. Even if you want to use all six plies in your embroidery, they should be separated and recombined. As the floss comes out of the skein, those six plies are wound round one another. If you don't separate the plies and get them to lie next to one another, your embroidery will look lumpy; your satin stitching, especially, will look bad.

Cut a working length of embroidery floss (no longer than 18") and hold in your left hand as illustrated above, with approximately ½" of the floss showing. Fluff the end of the floss by tapping on it with your right index finger. The plies will fan out (3.21b). While your left hand is firmly grasping the length of floss, use your right hand to pull out a single ply of

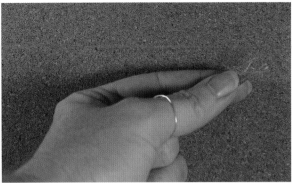

3.21a (left)

3.21b (right)

floss. If you want to use two strands for embroidery, strip out another ply. Even if you want to use all six strands, strip each ply and recombine them before threading into a needle. Now the threads will lie next to one another rather than wrap around one another.

I don't use a needle threader, those metal contrivances that have a wired loop on one end that you put through the eye of a needle, then insert your thread and pull the metal back through the eye. For sewing thread, I suppose it could work well enough. For various embroidery threads, however, I find them useless. I lick the end of my thread to put it into the needle. I find it eases the threading. Then, I cut off the licked portion of the thread. At first, I never thought it made a difference whether or not I cut that licked bit off. As I paid attention to whether my embroidery thread tangled or not, I noticed it was that licked bit that seemed to cause knots! Now, I avoid that extra entanglement by cutting the short portion of thread that was licked.

Needles are now made by stamping the piece of metal to make an eye, making one side of the eye more concave that the other. If you have difficulty threading the needle, try threading it from the other side, as it may be the more concave and, therefore, easier-to-thread side. It really makes a difference!

When stitching, if you are using a thin embroidery thread, such as floss, you can begin by using a knot to secure your thread. There may be times, however, when you want to use no knots at all. Satin fabrics show every little bump and lump and a knot will show as a lump under the fabric. You can use a tailor's tack to start your thread.

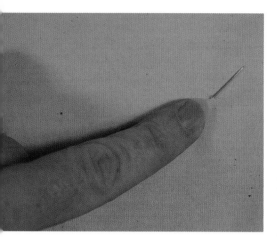

3.22

Have you ever accidentally stitched through a working bit of embroidery thread? It's nearly impossible to get that out! We are going to do that on purpose by working a tailor's tack (3.22).

Thread your needle, but do not knot the thread. Leaving a 4" tail, bring the needle up from under your fabric and take a teeny, tiny little straight stitch on top of the fabric. Remember, to leave that tail of thread underneath the fabric!! Your needle is now underneath the fabric again. Hold the tail of thread securely between your left thumb and the fabric to prevent it from working loose as you carefully bring the needle up through the fabric on the bottom and THROUGH the teeny, tiny straight stitch you made on top of the fabric, actually splitting the embroidery thread. This locks the thread in place. Try it out. Hold the needle and floss and let the fabric hang down. It is secure. Work a few stitches with the embroidery floss, then go back and trim the tail down to ⅛" or so.

Ending Your Embroidery Thread with Tension, Knot, Tension

You can end embroidery threads with a simple knot. Some will use a quilter's knot, if they come to crazy quilting through quilting and not embroidery. The problem with a quilter's knot is that, over time, the thread can work loose and have too much slack that then works to the front of the embroidery, creating loose stitches. A "spit" knot, where you twist the thread between thumb and index finger, is a little more secure, but can leave a lump. I remedied those problems by ending off with tension, knot, tension.

After completing the embroidery motif or stem, bring your needle and thread to the back of your work. Take a small bite of the muslin with your needle and pull through. Do not go through the fancy fabric on front of your work. This first "tension" stitch ensures the last stitch on the front of the work sits tightly against the fabric. Take another small bite of the muslin and this time, before pulling the thread completely through, slip the needle through the loop that forms, then pull through firmly. This forms a knot without a lump. Now, another tension stitch is needed so the tail of the knot doesn't work loose. So, take another little bite of the muslin and pull through. Cut the thread right up close to where the thread is exiting the muslin. This creates a very secure ending that won't come undone and provides tension on the front to keep the embroidery always looking neat and pretty.

Stem Stitch & Variations

and what's the difference between stem stitch and outline stitch?

EARLY EVERY antique crazy quilt contains motifs done in stem stitch, perhaps one of the most utilized stitches in embroidery. Stem stitch is used in redwork embroidery, which has enjoyed a revival in quilting. Any outline graphic can be done in this stitch; wording is also nicely done in fine stem stitch with a single strand of floss (4.1). In addition, spiderwebs can be worked in stem stitch with a fine metallic thread (4.2). I like to use Madeira #40 weight metallic machine thread for spiderwebs, even though I do the stitching by hand. I find this thread does not kink or break like some metallic threads meant for handwork.

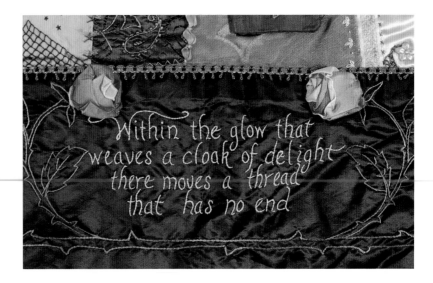

4.1

Stem stitch. Outline stitch. What's the difference and does it matter? There is a difference between these two stitches, although most people would be hard-pressed to understand that distinction once the stitch is completed. Stem stitch is worked with the thread always held down. Outline stitch is worked with the thread always held up. The KEY is consistency! No matter what other embroidery books tell you, do not switch from stem to outline stitch within one motif. Many authors recommend flipping your thread from down to up when going around a curve. *No!* This causes an uneven line in your stitching. ALWAYS stay consistent. If you stem stitch, always stem stitch. If you outline stitch, always outline stitch. Allow me to illustrate.

Bring the threaded needle up through the fabric. Take a small scoop of the fabric from right to left, making sure the needle shares the same hole in which you originally brought it up. This is the ONLY time you will position the needle so (4.3a).

Holding the thread down with your left thumb (down means you are doing stem stitch), take a small scoop of the fabric from right to left, making sure the needle shares the same hole as the right-hand side of the previous stitch. Be sure to watch this needle placement and stitch like this thoughout the remainder of the stem stitch (4.3b).

Pull thread through. Notice where the thread is exiting the fabric (4.3c). It may look as though you stitched halfway back from the previous stitch, but that is not how the stitch was done. You achieved this look when you placed your needle in the same hole as the right-hand side of the previous stitch. Most embroidery books show this incorrectly.

Hold the thread down (because this is stem stitch) and make the next stitch by taking a small scoop of the fabric from right to left, again making sure the needle shares the same hole as the right-hand side of the previous stitch (4.3d).

Continue (4.3e).

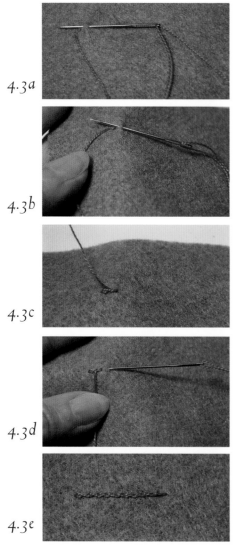

4.3a

4.3b

4.3c

4.3d

4.3e

These directions give the INCORRECT way of doing stem stitch; I include these so you can understand the difference. Bring needle up. Take a scoop of fabric from right to left, coming up in the same hole in which you originally brought up the needle (4.4a).

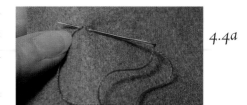

4.4a

Take a scoop of the fabric, from right to left. Instead of sharing the right-hand side of the previous stitch, go back halfway on top of the previous stitch. Pull thread through (4.4b). Continue across.

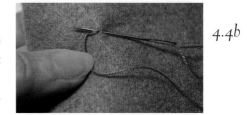

4.4b

This stitch (which can be useful when you want a thicker line) is not stem stitch. It is bulky and almost ropelike. Some Victorians called it Kensington stitch (4.4c).

4.4c

Compare the difference between stem stitch, on the top, and Kensington stitch, on the bottom (4.4d). They were both done with the same thread and needle. You can see why a properly stitched stem stitch lends itself more readily to redwork, embroidered writing, and other motifs in embroidery on crazy quilts.

4.4d

Bring the threaded needle up through the fabric. Take a small scoop of the fabric from right to left, making sure the needle shares the same hole in which you originally brought up the needle. This is the ONLY time you will position the needle so (4.5a).

Notice, however, that the thread is being kept UP.

Holding the thread UP with your left thumb, take a small scoop of the fabric from right to left, making sure the needle shares the same hole as the right-hand side of the previous stitch. Take care to watch this needle placement and stitch like this throughout the remainder of the stem stitch (4.5b).

Hold the thread up (because it is outline stitch) and make the next stitch by taking a small scoop of the fabric from right to left and making sure the needle shares the same hole as the right-hand side of the previous stitch. Continue (4.5c).

The only caveat is if you are doing stem stitch, always do stem stitch. Or, if you are doing outline stitch, always do outline stitch. Look what happens when you switch from stem to outline in the middle of the row (4.5d). Can you see the "hiccup" in the second line of stitching?

Below, left to right:
4.5a, 4.5b, 4.5c, 4.5d

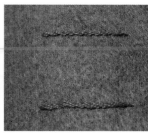

4.6

Threaded Stem Stitch

Work a row of stem stitch. Thread up with a contrasting color. Bring the needle up slightly to the left and top of where the stem stitch started. Working just under the stem stitch and NOT through the fabric, bring the needle up from below the next stem stitch and pull it through gently. Slide the needle under the next stem stitch from top to bottom. Pull it through gently. Slide the needle under the next stem stitch from bottom to top. Pull it through (4.6).

Continue across (4.7).

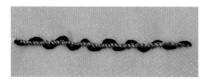

4.7

Whipped Stem Stitch

Work a row of stem stitch. Thread up in a contrasting color. Bring the needle up slightly to the left and top of where the stem stitch started. Working just under the stem stitch and NOT through the fabric, bring the needle up from below the next stem stitch and pull it through gently. Slide the needle under the next stem stitch from bottom to top (4.8).

Continue across (4.9).

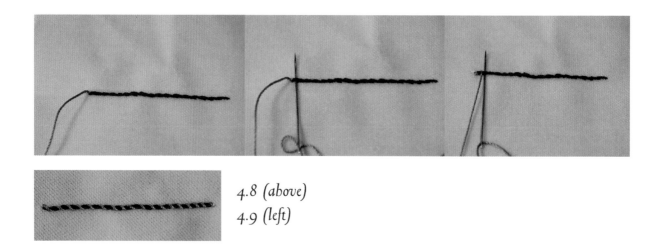

4.8 (above)
4.9 (left)

Motifs for Stem Stitch, Chain Stitch, or Other Ideas

As I stated earlier, flowers have always been popular subjects for embroidery and quilting. Figure 4.10 illustrates several floral motifs.

4.10

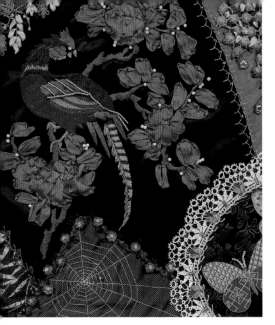

Spiderwebs appear often on Victorian crazy quilts. It has been speculated that they were embroidered as a symbol of good luck. In Greek mythology, Arachne was a weaver who had the audacity to challenge the goddess Athena, to a contest. When Arachne won, Athena, in a jealous rage, destroyed her tapestry. In despair, Arachne hung herself, but Athena took pity, restoring her to life, as a spider. So, beware of your talents!!

I like to use Madeira metallic machine thread #40 weight to stitch spiderwebs. This thread doesn't kink and break, as do so many other metallic threads. It is also fine enough to look like the gossamer strands of a web. I use stem stitch for the spokes of the web and either a straight stitch or a stem stitch for the strands between spokes.

4.11

4.12

4.13

5

Blanket Stitch & Variations

Blanket stitch is a useful stitch for bordering a quilt or for use along patches and seam lines. In figure 5.1, the blue stitching around the appliquéd hexagon is blanket stitch with French knots added.

Blanket stitch can be worked left to right or right to left. It can also be worked toward you or away from you. I like to work blanket stitch from left to right with the "fingers" of the stitch pointing down. I find this keeps my wrist in the most neutral position, resulting in less fatigue. Find which direction is best suited to you.

5.1

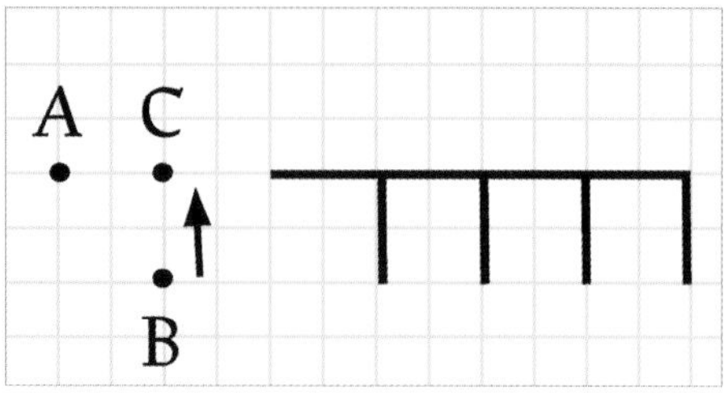

5.2

Some quilters have difficulty starting blanket stitch. They feel they should start with a lazy daisy stitch or a straight stitch to get going. That's because they aren't sure where to bring up the needle. If you bring it up below the seam line, it feels like you need a compensating stitch to get going. If you remember to start your blanket stitch ON the seam line and not below the seam line, you won't need to do a lazy daisy or straight stitch to start.

Blanket stitch can be worked left to right or right to left. Here it is being worked from left to right. Bring needle up at A—ON THE SEAM-LINE. Advance to the right. Insert needle at B and scoop up at C, keeping the thread under the tip of the needle. Pull the thread through (5.2).

5.3a

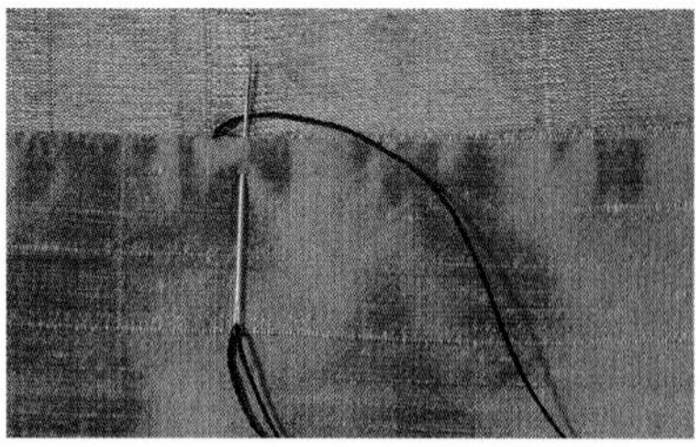

5.3b

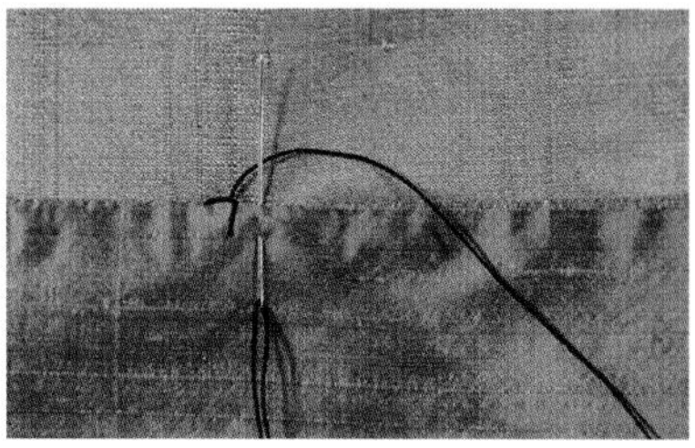

The point where the thread is emerging becomes the new point A. Advance to the right. Insert the needle at B and scoop up at C, keeping the thread under the tip of the needle(5.3a). Pull the thread through. Continue across the seam (5.3b).

Notice that the fingers of the blanket stitch hang down. A ridged line forms along the seam line (5.4).

5.4

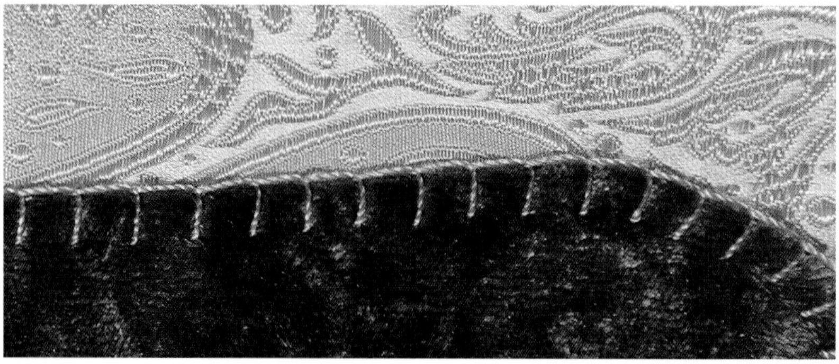

5.5

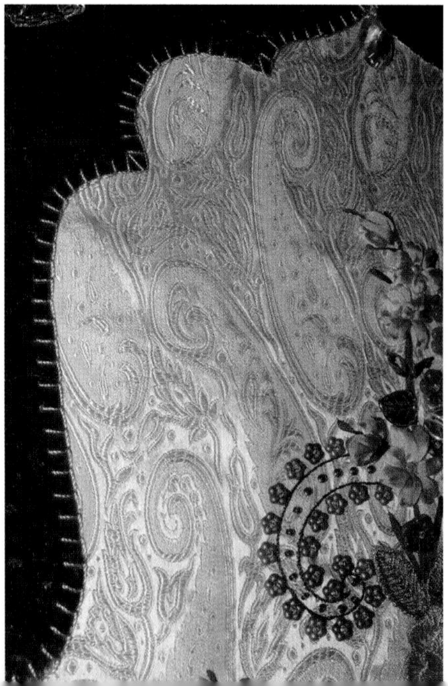

You could also have the fingers of the blanket stitch go the opposite way, to grasp the seam line. The blue stitching in figure 5.6 shows this. Instead of bringing the needle up on the seam line, bring the needle up above the seam line. Move to the right: point B would be on the seam line, and point C is above the seam line, evenly across from point A.

I added a pink fly stitch below the seam line.

5.6

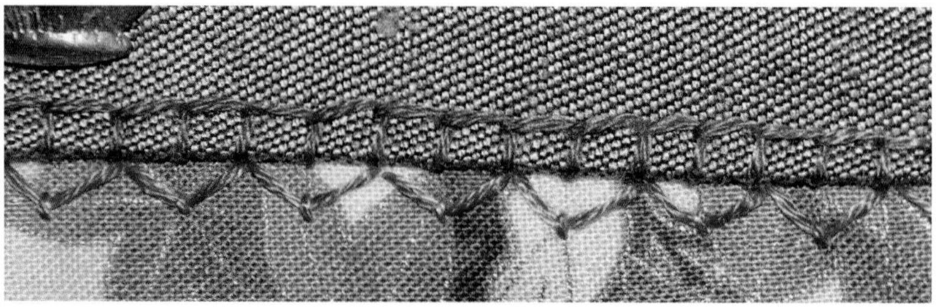

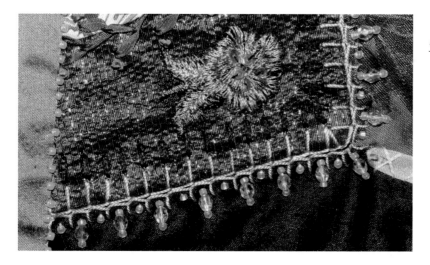

An alternative is to work blanket stitches back-to-back, with fingers going away from one another (5.7).

To accomplish this, I worked the first row of blanket stitch with the variegated pink thread. Then, I flipped the work 180 degrees and stitched with the green thread. I kept the spacing the same as the first round. I added beads and lazy daisies for more interest.

Another approach is to have the fingers enmeshed. Stitch the fingers going one way on the first pass. Change colors and the direction of the fingers for the second pass (5.8).

5.9

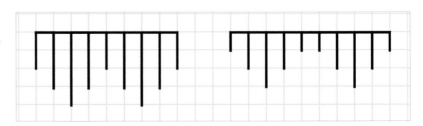

5.10

For variety, you can vary the length of the fingers of blanket stitch (5.9), or pack the stitches closer together or further apart (5.10).

"Shadow" a blanket stitch by working a second row in a different color just slightly to the left of the first blanket stitch (5.11).

5.11

To work a curve in blanket stitch, think of a folded fan opening. The blades of a fan are further apart at the outside curve of the fan than they are at the pivot point of a fan. The inside of the curve represents the pivot point of a fan; the stitches there are closer together. You can use a stencil of drafting circles to draw your curves on the fabric. or use a scrapbooking stencil for curves. Look at the outer border of the orange stencil on page 55, perfect for curves (3.20).

Work a curve (5.12).

In figure 5.13, the blue French knots were added after the blanket stitch was completed. Note how the curves are appearing above and below the seam line and going across several patches.

5.12

5.13

Pink French knots were added to the green curved blanket stitch. The purple blanket stitch had French knots, straight stitches, and decorated lazy daisies added. That's a bullion rose in the center (5.14).

5.14

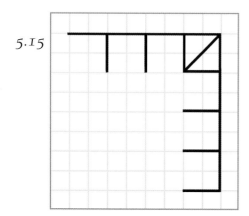

5.15

To make a sharp corner with blanket stitch, three stitches must share a pivot point on the inside. On the outside, stitch one is almost to the corner. Stitch two is on the corner itself. Stitch three rounds the corner. Now continue working a blanket stitch as usual (5.15).

To form a sharp corner, the three stitches at the corner share the inside hole.

Make several blanket stitches as you approach the corner (5.16a). Notice that I have turned the direction of my stitching at the corner. The needle is inserted in the same hole at the inside corner as the last blanket stitch, the tip comes up AT the corner, keeping the thread under the tip of the needle (5.16b).

The third stitch in the corner again shares the hole at the inside corner with the last two stitches. The tip of the needle comes up on the seam line, keeping the thread under the tip of the needle (5.17a). Continue to blanket stitch across the seam. You have a nice squared corner (5.17b).

Note the corner and the sharing hole of the three stitches. Three beads were then added to every other finger of the blanket stitch (5.18).

5.16a

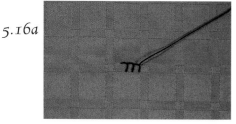

5.16b

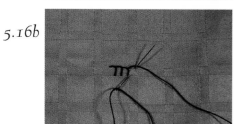

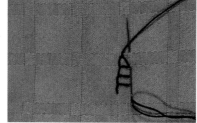

5.17a

5.17b

5.18

You can work a circle in blanket stitch (5.19). Use the drafting circle stencil or, if you prefer, the scrapbooking stencil to draw your circles. If you find your stitches flop along the outside edge, make your stitches closer together. Also, don't pack all your inside stitches in the exact same hole in the center of the circle. This creates a large hole in the fabric. Rather, cluster the inside stitches around a wee small circle in the center. When you are finished stitching, that wee small circle in the center will look like one hole, without creating a hole in the fabric...

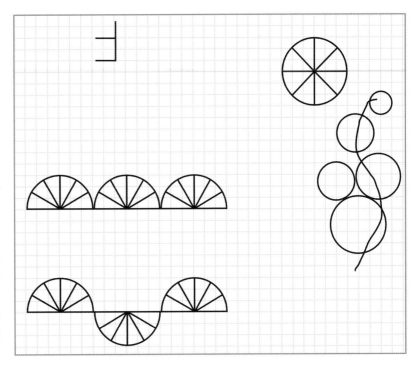

If the thread flops on the outside, make your stitches closer together. Make half circles for fans. Alternate the half circles along a seam line for lots of movement.

5.19

In figure 5.20, a yellow French knot was added to the center of these blanket stitch circles, creating hollyhocks!

5.20

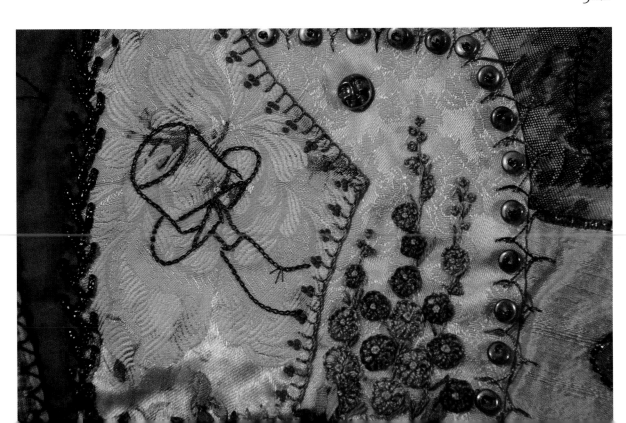

Alternating half-circle blanket stitches with beads added in the centers are worked along a seam (5.21).

Half-circle blanket stitches have crystals sewn between each stitch (5.22).

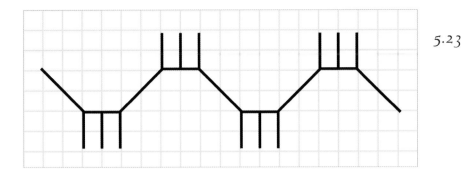

Antique Blanket Stitch

I see this stitch on many vintage crazy quilts: sometimes with three fingers each way, sometimes with more fingers (5.23). Note: to achieve the zigzag effect, the top stitches are placed above the seam line, with the bottom stitches below the seam line. Afterwards, bullion-tipped lazy daisies, straight stitches, and fly stitches were embroidered (5.24).

This antique blanket stitch was worked with two fingers in each direction with a variegated thread. I then sewed on glass hearts in the empty spaces below the seam line (5.25).

5.24

5.25

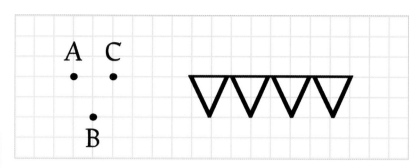

5.26

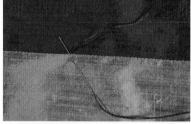

5.27a

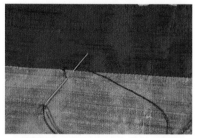

5.27b

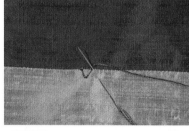

5.27c

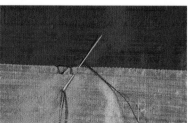

5.27d

Closed Blanket Stitch

This stitch is really lovely along a seam, especially if you have one fabric that is thicker than the adjoining fabric (5.26). It provides a way to bridge that gap without looking like you have done so.

Bring the needle up on the seam line at point A. Pull the thread through. Insert the needle into B and scoop up at A, keeping the thread under the tip of the needle (5.27a). Pull the thread through. Insert the needle at B and scoop up at C, keeping the thread under the tip of the needle (5.27b). Pull the thread through. C now becomes point A of the next stitch. Continue across seam.

Note how the tip of the needle first swings to the left and then to the right. However, where you insert the needle, at the point of the triangle, is a shared hole (5.27c). Keep the thread under the tip of the needle as shown (5.27d).

French knots have been added to the point of the closed blanket stitch. Flower beads have been added to the top of the seam (5.28).

5.28

74

5.29

Work a row of closed blanket stitch and then add straight stitches to make shadowing (5.29).

Alternate blanket stitch and closed blanket stitch have French knots at the points and blanket stitch below (5.30).

Alternate blanket stitch and closed blanket stitch are embellished with chenille French knots and beads (5.31).

5.30

5.31

Herringbone Stitch
& Variations

H ERRINGBONE STITCH has been used historically to hem linings in coats and dresses. But, aside from its utilitarian component, herringbone is also a lovely embroidery stitch. This beautiful stitch works wonderfully well in crazy quilting. Herringbone can straddle a seam line (6.1a), be worked above or below a seam line, or meander artistically throughout a patch (6.1b).

6.1a

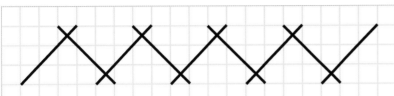

6.3a

6.3b

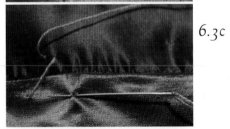

6.3c

6.3d

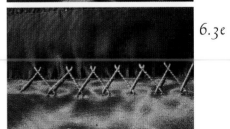

6.3e

Herringbone stitch (6.2) is worked from left to right. It can be started above or below the seam line, as desired. For this demonstration, I am starting below the seam line.

Bring the threaded needle up below the seam line. Visually, advance to the right (6.3a).

Go above the seam line. Insert needle, taking a scoop of the fabric from right to left. Let the thread trail behind the needle. Because you are taking a scoop of the fabric, your hand stays above the fabric; it does not go underneath the fabric. Do not stab down through the fabric and reach underneath to grab the needle. Keep your hand on top and just insert the tip of the needle into and out of the cloth in one smooth motion. Draw needle completely through (6.3b).

Advance to the right. Come up below the seam line. Insert needle, taking a scoop of the fabric from right to left. Let the thread trail behind the needle (6.3c). Continue advancing to the right with each stitch, alternating above and below the seam.

Continue advancing to the right with each stitch, alternating coming up above and below the seam line (6.3d).

You have now completed a herringbone seam (6.3e).

HERRINGBONE STITCH & VARIATIONS

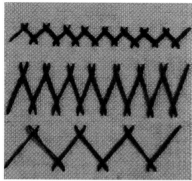

6.4

Herringbone can change its look by being very regular, by varying its height, or by varying its spacing (6.4).

Herringbone can be worked over a ribbon—in this case, a velvet ribbon (6.5). Sew the ribbon down. Then, work a herringbone stitch on top. This time, I went off the ribbon and took the scoop of the background fabric. After completing the herringbone, I made the French knots and added the bugle beads.

Herringbone can be worked in successive rows (6.6). Stitch one row below another.

Herringbone can be done in two colors. I stitched the first pass with yellow silk floss. The second pass was stitched with white silk floss and was worked in the empty spaces. Notice how nicely herringbone works along a curved patch (6.7).

6.6

6.7

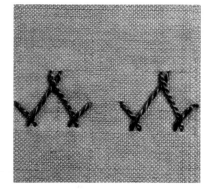

This row of herringbone, worked above a seam, was done with silk ribbon (6.8). The stitch looks quite rustic when worked with a thicker thread. Ribbon stitches and twisted bugle beads were added.

I call this stitch interrupted herringbone (6.9). I start at the seam line. Go below the seam line and take a herringbone stitch, go above the seam line and take a herringbone stitch, then go below the seam line and take another herringbone stitch, ending on the seam line. Leave a space and complete another section.

Herringbone can be tied. Work the herringbone seam with one color. With a second color, go through and make a straight stitch where the herringbone makes a X. I used blue to tie down the herringbone (6.10a). Figure 6.10b shows a row of herringbone worked in gold-colored thread, then tied at top and bottom with a contrasting color.

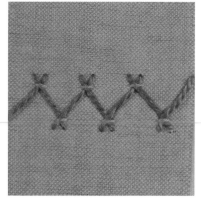

6.11 (above)

6.12 (right)

Figure 6.11 shows tied herringbone worked with Rachel thread (rather like a tube of nylon). It was tied with two strands of silk floss. This approach gives the stitch quite a different look. Lazy daisies were added afterwards.

For the seam in figure 6.12, I worked the green herringbone. Next, I went back and worked the pink herringbone. I tied the top and bottom with straight stitches in pink. I then used a metallic thread to tie the central portion with a +.

Woven Herringbone

To create a woven herringbone stitch, work a row of herringbone as usual. (I used variegated purple/brown floss.) For the second row, you will work a different color in the spaces between (I used pink pearl silk), with one difference: when you go from below to above the seam, before you take the scoop of the fabric above, make sure you slide the needle underneath the previous row's stitch. This puts the pink underneath the purple (6.13).

6.13

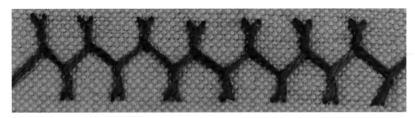

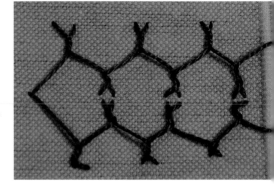

Twisted Herringbone

The twisted herringbone stitch begins the same as regular herringbone (6.14). Come up at the bottom and bring the thread all the way through. Advance to the right, go to the top of the seam and take a scoop of the fabric from right to left, letting the thread trail behind you. Now comes the difference. Instead of advancing to the right and dropping below the seam line, you will instead scoop under the stitch you just made, from right to left, as shown in figure 6.15. Note that the needle and thread DO NOT go through the fabric at this point. You are just sliding the needle between the herringbone stitch and the fabric. Pull the needle and thread completely under. The stitch will seem slightly loose at this point. That's okay; you will tighten the tension by completing the next part of the stitch.

Next, continue as though you were stitching regular herringbone by advancing to the right and dropping down below the seam line, taking a small scoop of the fabric from right to left. Pull the thread completely through the fabric. You will notice that by taking this part of the stitch, the previous herringbone stitch is now twisted and the tension is tight. If the tension is not as tight as you would like, tug slightly on the thread.

Slide your needle under the stitch you just made, from right to left. Remember to just go under the thread, not through the fabric (6.16).

Continue along the seam, always advancing to the right and alternating above and below the seam line. Remember to twist the herringbone stitch by sliding the needle under the thread before advancing to the next stitch.

If you put two rows of twisted herringbone stacked upon one another (6.17), it looks like chicken wire!

This twisted herringbone, done in pink pearl cotton, was enlivened by fairy charms and lazy daisies (6.18).

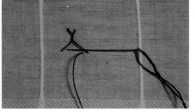

6.17

6.18

6.19

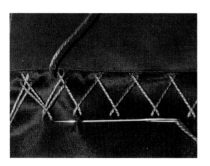

6.20a

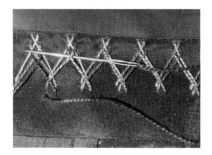

6.20b

Shadow Herringbone

I don't know if this stitch's real name is shadow herringbone. I stitched it and that's what I call it. I worked herringbone across as I normally would. I then stitched a second row, in a slightly darker color (6.19). Notice where the scoop of fabric in the second row is placed (6.20a). Instead of scooping below the X of the previous herringbone stitch, I scooped AT the X, making it look as though the second row of herringbone is hugging the first row, or shadowing it.

You could add a third row, if desired, as I did (6.20b). Notice that I am using increasingly darker pearl cotton colors for interest.

Interlaced Herringbone

Interlaced herringbone can be a very interesting stitch, depending on which threads are used. In figure 6.21, interlaced herringbone was worked over a copper ribbon with pink pearl silk for the herringbone and black #8 metallic braid for the interlacing. Black 4 mm crystals were sewn on after the stitching.

Figure 6.22 shows interlaced herringbone with pink pearl cotton for the herringbone and white pearl cotton for the interlacing. Crystals and pearl seed beads were added after the stitching.

6.21

6.22

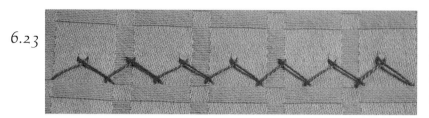

6.23

To stitch interlaced herringbone, work the first row of herringbone in a thread of your choice, I used #8 pearl cotton and spaced the tops of the herringbones about ½" apart (6.23).

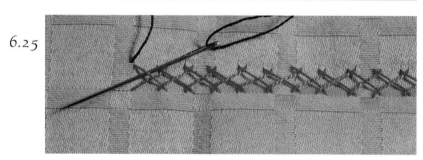

6.24

Then, stitch a second row of herringbone to fill in the spaces of the first row (6.24).

To interlace the herringbone, choose a new thread that will be long enough to go across the entire seam. In figure 6.25, I used a contrasting color, the purple silk pearl. Bring the thread up just to the left at the top of your first herringbone stitch. Now, all the interlacing will be done by weaving the needle under the herringbone stitches; you will not go back through the fabric until you reach the end of the seam.

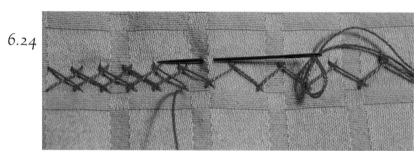

6.25

Slide the needle from top to bottom under the first diagonal \ of the first herringbone stitch and bring the thread completely through.

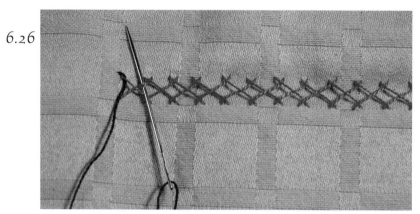

6.26

Now, skip across and slide the needle up under the / of the herringbone. Pull the thread all the way through (6.26).

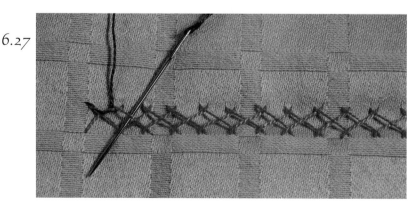

6.27

Slide the needle under the next \ of the herringbone stitch. Continue across the row (6.27).

When you get to the end of the row, it will look like this (6.28).

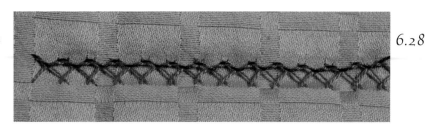
6.28

Now, flip your work upside down so you are once again working from left to right. Bring the thread up just to the left at the top of your first herringbone. All the interlacing will be done by weaving the needle under the herringbone stitches; you will not go back through the fabric until you reach the end of the seam (6.29).

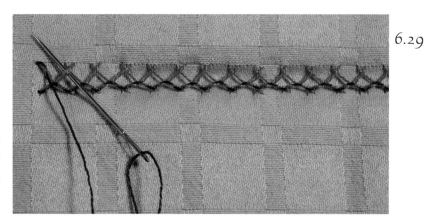
6.29

Slide the needle from top to bottom under the first diagonal \ of the first herringbone stitch and bring the thread completely through (6.30).

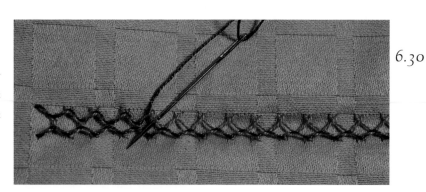
6.30

Now, skip across and slide the needle up under the / of the herringbone. Pull the thread all the way through (6.31).

Continue across the seam as you did for the first section.

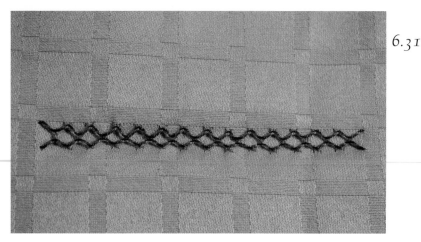
6.31

Herringbone can also be worked rather organically, flowing in a more natural way. Figure 6.32 shows a stitched spiral worked with herringbone. I started in the center and worked in a spiral, gradually increasing the size and spacing of the herringbone. I did not worry about being exact.

This seam started with four rows of herringbone with the last row spilling out to form its own spiral (6.33). I then added another row of herringbone forming from the spiral to continue on its own. The beauty of crazy quilting is that you can be as exacting and regimented as you like. You may also create very organic and free-flowing stitches if you desire.

6.32

6.33

Cretan Stitch & Variations

CRETAN STITCH, so named due to its origin on the Greek island of Crete, has been used for centuries in embroidery and other needlework. This versatile stitch can be used to create lovely borders, to surround embellishments, or to fill in line motifs. To me, Cretan stitch looks like gothic arches. I love how Cretan stitch flows across a seam line and provides plenty of room to add embellishments, as in figure 7.1a. Multicolored Cretan stitch is adorned with blue lazy daisies and cream beads. Underneath the seam, I placed a brass hand ornament holding silk ribbon rosebuds.

7.1a

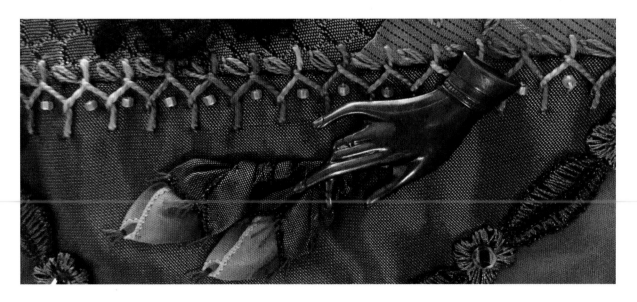

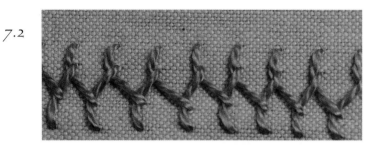

7.1b

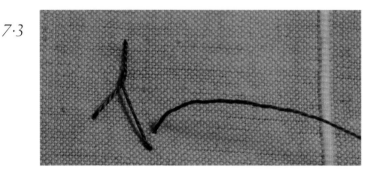

7.2

7.3

To learn Cretan stitch (7.1b), it is very helpful to have learned herringbone stitch. The rhythm of the stitches is the same: Always advance to the right. If you are above the seam, drop below to take the stitch; if you are below the seam, go above to take the stitch. The difference is in how you scoop into the fabric. With herringbone, the scoop is made horizontally, from right to left. With Cretan, the scoop is down vertically, always pointing to the seam line. Therefore, if you are stitching above the seam line, take a scoop from top to bottom, with the tip of the needle pointing toward the seam line. With Cretan stitch, you must always keep the thread under the tip of the needle!! Pull the thread through (7.2).

When you are coming up below the seam line, you scoop from bottom to top, always keeping the thread under the tip of the needle.

If your stitches have a gap, you did not keep the thread under the tip of the needle as you pulled the thread through (7.3).

It doesn't matter if you start from above or below a seam. In figure 7.4a, the thread starts below the seam. Advance to the right. Go above the seam line. Take a scoop from top to bottom, keeping the thread under the tip of the needle. Pull through.

Advance to the right. Drop down below the seam line. Take a scoop from bottom to top, keeping the thread under the tip of the needle. Pull through (7.4b).

Continue across the seam line by alternating stitches above and below the seam line (7.4c).

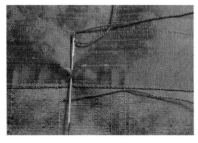

7.4a

7.4b

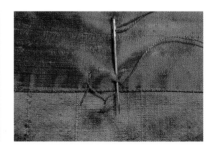

7.4c

CRAZY QUILTS

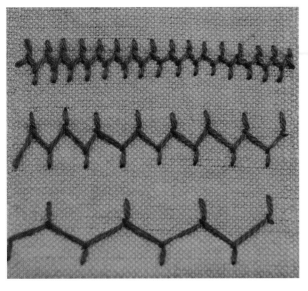

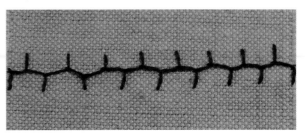

This first row of Cretan stitch shows the stitches evenly spaced (7.5a).

Vary the look by spacing the stitches out a bit (second row).

Cretan stitch looks very different when you space the stitch out even more (third row).

To achieve this look (7.5b), don't go above or below the seam line very far. The stitch will flatten out and almost look like a blanket stitch.

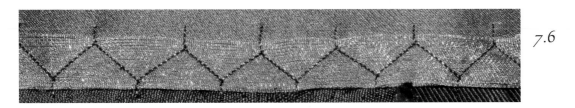

7.6

I tacked an organza ribbon in place and then used a fine metallic thread to work Cretan stitch across (7.6). I made sure the scoops of the Cretan stitch caught the organza so it was firmly held in place.

7.7

Figure 7.7 shows two rows of Cretan stitch worked so they slightly intermesh.

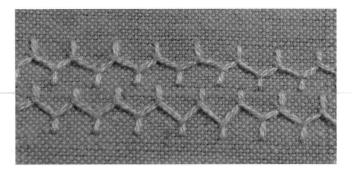

CRETAN STITCH & VARIATIONS

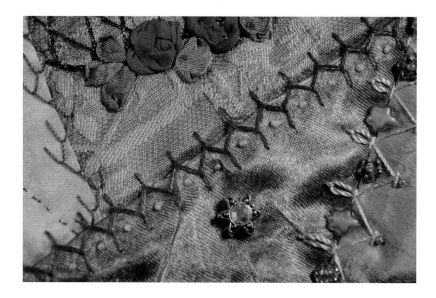

For this look (7.8), I used two threads in the needle at the same time and stitched Cretan as I normally would.

Two passes of Cretan stitch are shown here (7.9). For the first row, I stitched in blue thread. Then, I used pink thread, working in the spaces between the first Cretan stitch row.

I used Rachel thread for this seam and added bugle beads after the Cretan stitch was completed (7.10).

7.10

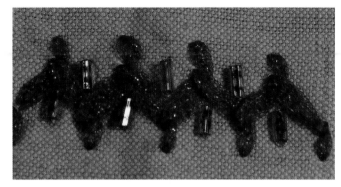

For this seam (7.11), I took a bigger scoop of the fabric above the seam. Then, with green thread, I added lazy daisies to that big scoop.

7.11

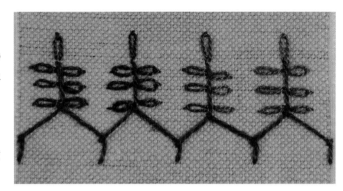

For this seam (7.12), you will notice that the Cretan stitch is placed slightly differently along the seam line; only the bottom scoop is actually below the seam line. Then, I added French knots, straight stitches, and lazy daisies.

7.12

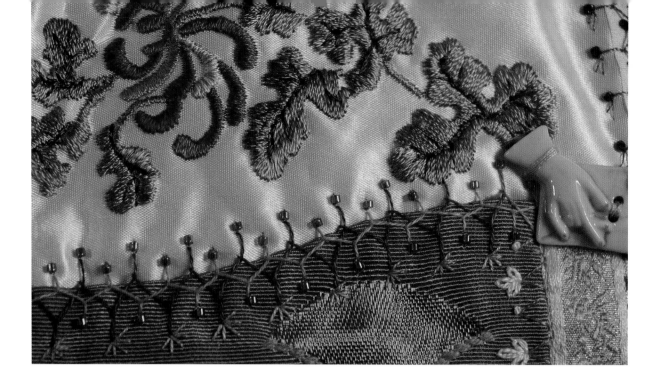

Figure 7.13 shows two passes of Cretan stitch, but with differing heights. The first pass, in blue thread, was done with the top scoop resting on the seam line. The second pass, in variegated pink thread, was stitched, but with a smaller scoop. Then straight stitches and beads were added.

This widely spaced Cretan stitch done in burgundy silk pearl has a cigarette silk interrupting its length (7.14). Notice how straight stitches and lazy daisies have been added below the seam, but not above.

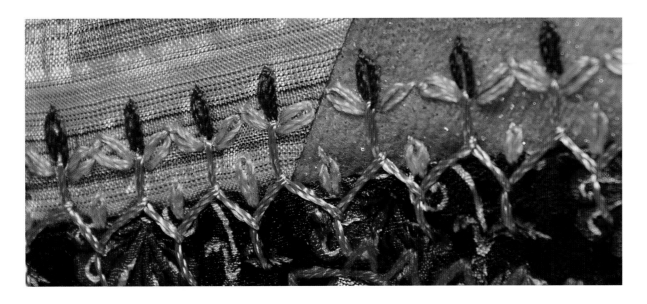

This Cretan stitch was done with rayon floss in pink (7.15). The lime green and dark blue lazy daisies add a punch of color.

To get around the corner of this dark blue patch, the Cretan stitch has been "squeezed" at the top to accommodate the angle (7.16).

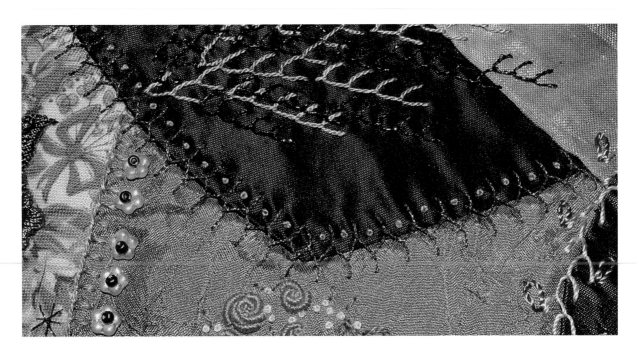

8

Chevron Stitch

a platform for decoration

 KNOWLEDGE OF herringbone stitch is helpful when learning another stitch, chevron. Chevron stitch follows the same rhythm as both herringbone and Cretan stitch: always advance to the right and alternate above and below the seam. Just a few differences make the straight stitch that becomes a platform on which decorative elements can be added.

8.1

You can start above or below the seam line. This time I am starting below the seam line. Bring the thread up below the seam line (8.2a).

Advance to the right and scoop a stitch right to left above the seam line. Pull through (8.2b).

The stitch looks like this (8.2c).

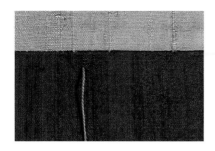
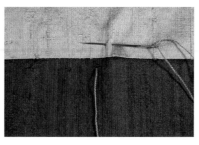
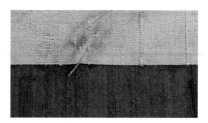

8.2a (left)
8.2b (center)
8.2c (right)

Make sure the working thread is above your work, out of your way, as you take a scoop of the fabric from right to left, bringing the point of the needle up to share the hole in the middle (8.3a).

Pull the thread through. Notice the position of the thread (8.3b).

The thread has been pulled through. Note the "bar" on top of the stitch. To progress for the next stitch, advance to the right (8.3c).

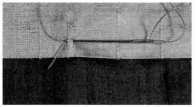
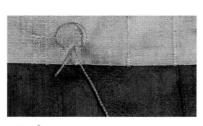
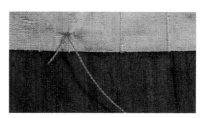

8.3a　　　　　*8.3b*　　　　　*8.3c*

8.3d

Go below the seam, and take a little scoop of the fabric from right to left. Pull thread through (8.3d).

Take a scoop of the fabric from right to left, sharing the same hole where the thread went in previously. Pull through (8.4a).

Advance to the right. Go above the seam and take a little stitch from right to left. Continue (8.4b).

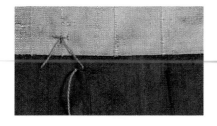

8.4a (far left)
8.4b (left)

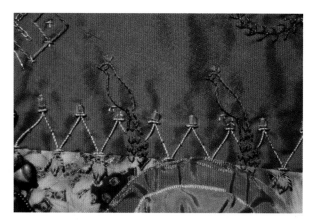

8.5

Because chevron stitch forms the great bar at the top and bottom of the stitch, it provides a terrific platform for added embroidery, beads, and other adornments. Figure 8.5 shows an idea that I adapted from a piece by Christine Dabbs. Peacocks perch on chevron stitches that have been couched. Beads sit on the otherwise empty platforms.

8.6

I worked two rows of chevron stitches (8.6). I stitched the green row first. Then, a little to the right and slightly below the original row, I placed a pink row.

To make shadows, I first worked a row of chevron stitches. Then, I added blue straight lines on either side of the chevron stitches. I added French knots and straight lines in green for interest (8.7a).

8.7a

8.8

8.7b

Figure 8.9 shows how chevron stitch can be worked around a curve. Note how the stitches are closer on the inside of the curve and further apart on the outside of the curve. Decorated lazy daisies and straight stitches add interest.

8.9

Figure 8.10a shows chevron stitch worked with two strands of silk floss, then topped with beads. Straight stitches in variegated floss were added. Lazy daisies and straight stitches were added to the bottom platform.

In figure 8.10b, chevron stitch is done in white silk. Lime green lazy daisies are stitched on the top platform, beads on the bottom. In the spaces between, alternating star and flower beads were added.

Two passes of chevron stitches were done so they mirrored one another (8.10c). On the top row, straight stitches in blue and French knots in green were added. On the bottom row, couching stitches in light blue were added.

8.10c

Combination Stitches

achieving elegance

OW THAT you see how herringbone, Cretan, and chevron stitching share the same basic rhythms, differing only on where the needle is inserted into the fabric, you can begin to create combinations with these stitches, throwing in some blanket stitches for good measure. As you are combining stitches, remember to also combine threads. Combine silk threads with metallic, cotton with ribbon, and chunky with smooth.

In figure 9.1, antique blanket stitch has been worked in green floss in the first pass. Pink herringbone has been worked in the empty spaces in the second pass.

9.1

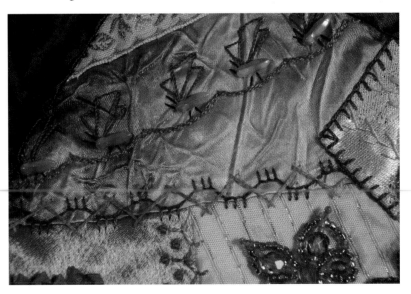

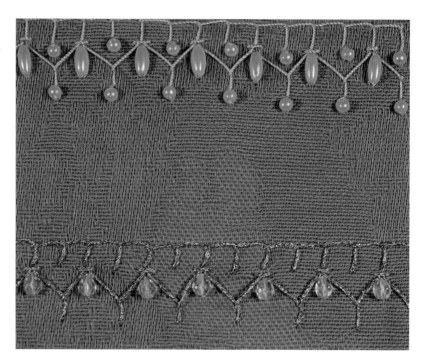

9.2a

9.2b

This seam is made by working a row of blanket stitch (9.2a, top). Then, another row is stitched with chevron on top and Cretan stitch on the bottom. Pearls and oat (rice) pearls were added.

Here's the same stitch done in metallic thread and with crystals rather than the pearls (9.2a, bottom).

Figure 9.2b shows the same seam treatment of blanket stitch on the first pass, then chevron and Cretan stitch. Instead of oat pearls or crystals, silk ribbon buds were added. Beads fill in every other space. Along the blanket stitch is another blanket stitch in a lighter color with the fingers going the opposite way.

Another variation of the same blanket stitch with the chevron/Cretan combination stitch is shown here, done in metallic thread (9.2c). Size 11 seed beads and crystals were added. Then, lazy daisies, straight stitches, and French knots were added above the blanket stitch.

9.2c

The seam toward the bottom of figure 9.3a shows the chevron/Cretan combination with clear flower beads, drop pearls, and seed beads added. Across the top of the chevron are more lazy daisies and straight stitches.

Figure 9.3b illustrates a herringbone and Cretan stitch combination. The stitching was done along opposite sides of a long patch (this would also work along a wide ribbon) so that the seams were mirrored. Note that the Cretan stitches go toward the center. Dragonfly charms and glass flower beads were added. Next came metallic lazy daisies, straight stitches, and French knots. Size 11 seed beads were added down the center.

9.3ª

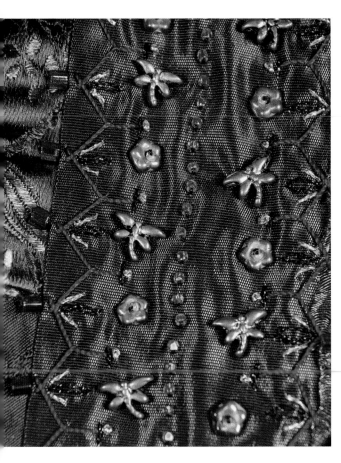

9.3ᵇ

9.4

The first row of this seam treatment was worked in the Cretan stitch in green, with extra-long stitches for the top (9.4). Next I placed the white straight stitches. I added the blue herringbone stitch next, taking up the spaces between the Cretan stitches. I then added white French knots. Finally, I placed pink lazy daisies along that extra-long Cretan stitch on the tip.

I created the seam to the right of the silk-ribbon iris with blue metallic herringbone stitching, tied with a lime green silk floss. I added single herringbone stitching in light blue in every other empty space. Pink lazy daisies cap the herringbone. I added antique nailhead beads along the bottom of the seam (9.5a).

9.5a

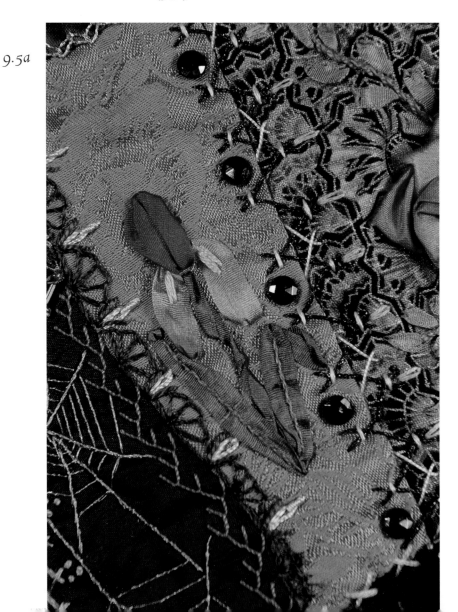

I appliquéd the fairy fabric, adding blanket stitches in a metallic thread, with the fingers facing the fairy. I then added another row of blanket stitches with the fingers facing out. The seam treatment is yellow silk with straight stitches along the top on the chevron platform and lazy daisies and French knots at the bottom of the Cretan stitches (9.5b).

9.6

In figure 9.6, antique blanket stitches with added gold beads are combined with straight stitches to form diamonds. French knots create the centers of the diamonds. Glass flower beads were attached with a seed bead forming the center. To the right of the fairy is a chevron stitch with French knots on the platform and straight stitches adding interest. Note the row of herringbone on the other side of that seam.

On the white and blue seam is a tied herringbone stitch with straight stitches forming starbursts.

Featherstitch & Variations

*you gotta fly before you can feather and
why "shoulder, shoulder, bellybutton"
means never marking a seam*

FEATHERSTITCH IS a chain of fly stitches. If you were to make a single featherstitch and end off, that is a fly stitch. Some embroidery books teach a triple featherstitch by telling you to start by drawing five parallel lines onto your fabric. Yikes! How would those lines get off the fabric when you are done embroidering? Then, you are supposed to line up the bottom of one stitch with the top of another. This method can get quite confusing. There is a simpler approach that does not involve marking your fabric.

IO.I

Have you ever heard the saying, "Watch the pennies and the dollars will look out for themselves?" The same rule applies to featherstitches—triple, quadruple, or quintuple. If you pay attention to each individual featherstitch (in reality, a fly stitch) and keep each one accurate, then the chain of stitches will automatically line up for you, without a need for marking!

To make a fly stitch, and, thereby, featherstitches, you need to remember where your shoulders and bellybutton are. Here's an illustration that may help (10.2).

This may seem silly, but it will help you visualize where the needle gets inserted into the fabric. (It will also make subsequent variations easier.) Let's say the distance between your shoulders is ¼". Let's say the distance between your shoulders and your bellybutton is halfway between your shoulders and ¼" down.

Come up at the left shoulder, bringing the thread all the way through. Insert needle at the right shoulder and scoop up at the bellybutton, keeping the thread under the tip of the needle (10.3a).

If you were to plunge down and take the needle to the back of the fabric, you would have a fly stitch. It should look like a little V (10.3b).

Fly stitches can line up with shoulders touching. To form the next fly stitch, bring the thread up at the next stitch's left shoulder. Insert needle at the right shoulder and scoop up at the bellybutton (10.3c).

Continue with a third fly stitch. You could stitch like this all the way across a seam line (10.3d).

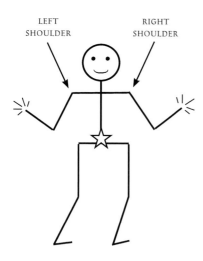

LEFT SHOULDER   RIGHT SHOULDER

10.2

10.3a (left)
10.3b (right)

10.3c (left)
10.3d (right)

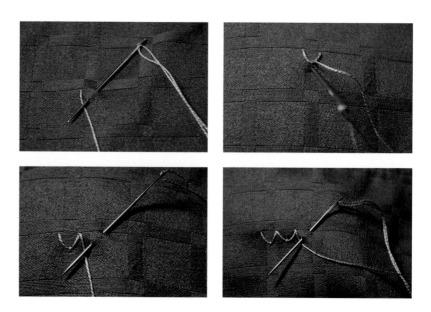

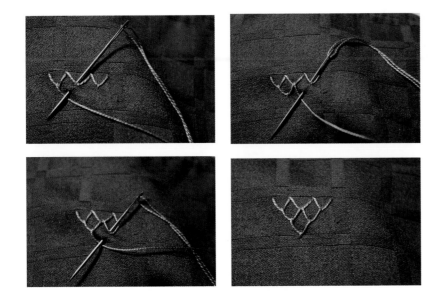

10.4*a (left)*
10.4*b (right)*

10.4*c (left)*
10.4*d (right)*

However, to form a pretty lace pattern, let's change things a little. Go back to the first fly stitch and bring the needle up at the bellybutton of that stitch. This will now be the left shoulder of the new fly stitch. Bring thread all the way through. Go over to the second fly stitch's bellybutton and insert your needle there (the new fly stitch's right shoulder). Scoop up at the new bellybutton. Plunge down through the fabric (10.4a).

Come up at the second fly stitch's bellybutton in the first row. This is the left shoulder. Bring the thread all the way through. Go down at the third stitch's bellybutton on the first row (new stitch's right shoulder). Scoop up at the new bellybutton. Plunge down through the fabric (10.4b).

For the third row, come up at the bellybutton of the first stitch in the second row (new left shoulder). Go down at the bellybutton of the second stitch in the second row (new right shoulder). Scoop up at the new bellybutton. Plunge down through the fabric (10.4c).

Figure 10.4d shows a completed lace design. This can be done all the way across a seam, along a motif, or to fill a patch that seems too plain, et cetera.

10.5*a*

10.5b

10.5c

Fly stitches can also line up one under another. Just line up all the shoulders—or not, as you desire.

This fly stitch line up is done in floss (10.6a).

This one is done with silk ribbon and a long tie-down stitch (10.6b).

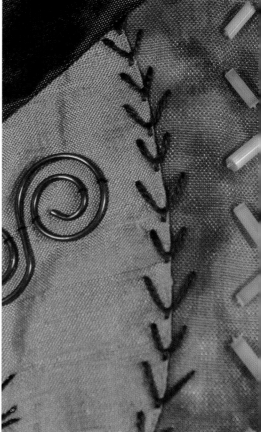

10.6a

10.6b

FEATHER   TRIPLE FEATHER   SINGLE FEATHER   DOUBLE SINGLE   DRUNKEN   MAIDENHAIR

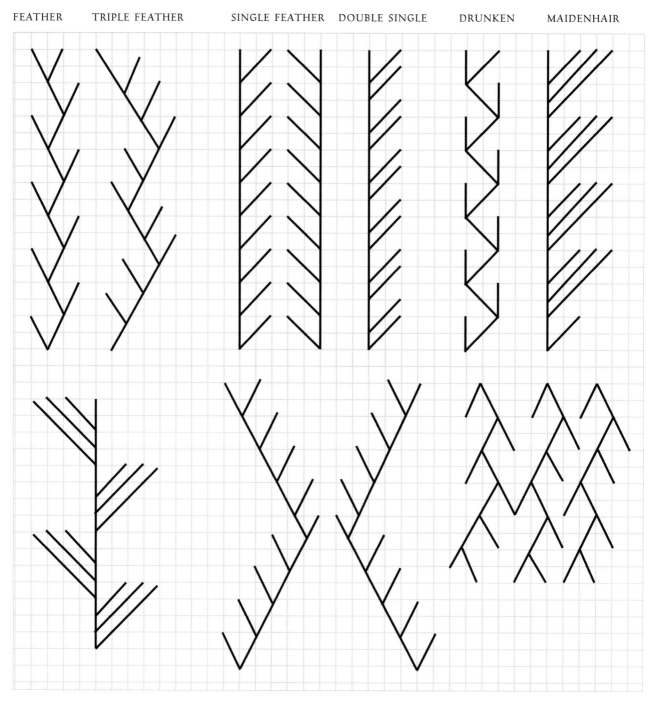

ALTERNATING MAIDENHAIR   QUINTUPLE FEATHERSTITCH   RAINING FEATHERS

Featherstitch

Featherstitch (10.7) is really the quintessential crazy-quilt embroidery stitch. Rare is the antique crazy quilt that does not have featherstitching of some sort on it. Refer back to chapter three, preparing for embroidery, to see how very different featherstitches can look, simply when done in different types of embroidery threads. Once you learn the basics, it is quite easy to stitch variations. It all depends on if you know where the shoulders, bellybuttons, and hips are!

Come up at the left shoulder, bringing the needle and thread all the way through. Insert the needle at the right shoulder and scoop up at the bellybutton, keeping the thread under the tip of the needle. Pull through (10.8a).

The bellybutton now becomes the left shoulder of the next stitch. Insert the needle at the right shoulder and scoop up at the bellybutton, keeping the thread under the tip of the needle. Pull through (10.8b).

To swing back to the left, the bellybutton now becomes the RIGHT shoulder of the next stitch. Insert the needle at the left shoulder and scoop up at the bellybutton, keeping the thread under the tip of the needle. Pull through (10.8c).

See how the featherstitch swings left, right, left. Now to go back to the right, this is no longer the bellybutton; it is now the left shoulder (10.8d).

Insert the needle at the right shoulder and scoop up at the bellybutton, keeping the thread under the tip of the needle. Pull through (10.8e).

Below, left to right:
10.8a, 10.8b, 10.8c

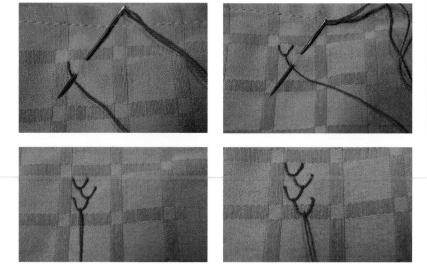

10.8d (left)
10.8e (right)

FEATHERSTITCH & VARIATIONS

111

10.9a

FEATHERSTITCH IN BEADS

10.9b

FEATHERSTITCH WITH LEAF BEADS

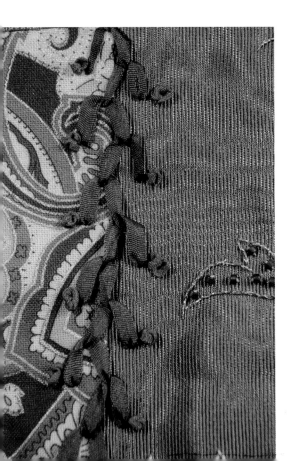

10.9c

FEATHERSTITCH WITH SILK RIBBON

10.10

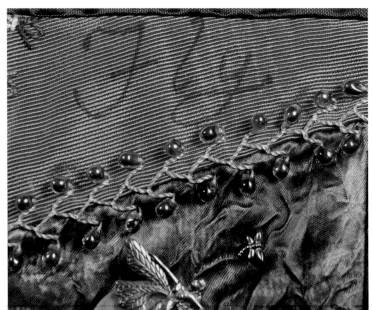

Triple Feather

Come up at the left shoulder, bringing the needle and thread all the way through. Insert the needle at the right shoulder and scoop up at the bellybutton, keeping the thread under the tip of the needle. Pull through (10.11a).

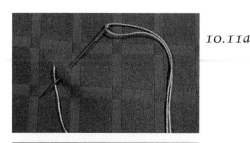

The bellybutton now becomes the left shoulder of the next stitch. Insert the needle at the right shoulder and scoop up at the bellybutton, keeping the thread under the tip of the needle. Pull through (10.11b).

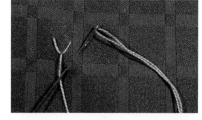

10.11b

The bellybutton now becomes the left shoulder of the next stitch. Insert the needle at the right shoulder and scoop up at the bellybutton, keeping the thread under the tip of the needle. Pull through (10.11c).
You now have three featherstitches going to the right. It's time to swing back to the left.

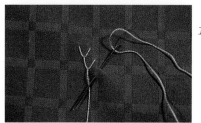

10.11c

The bellybutton now becomes the right shoulder of the next stitch. Insert the needle at the left shoulder and scoop up at the bellybutton, keeping the thread under the tip of the needle. Pull through (10.11d).

10.11d

Once more we will go to the left. The bellybutton now becomes the right shoulder of the next stitch. Insert the needle at the left shoulder and scoop up at the bellybutton, keeping the thread under the tip of the needle. Pull through (10.11e).

10.11e

To continue, work your way back to the right. Notice that the last stitch to the right becomes the first stitch going to the left. And the last stitch on the left becomes the first stitch going to the right (10.12).

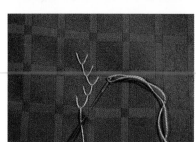

10.12

10.13b

TRIPLE FEATHER WITH CRYSTALS

10.13c

TRIPLE FEATHER WITH BULLION LAZY DAISY

10.13d

TRIPLE FEATHER AS A BORDER
TREATMENT ON THE LEFT,
CRETAN STITCH ON THE RIGHT

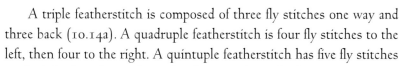

A triple featherstitch is composed of three fly stitches one way and three back (10.14a). A quadruple featherstitch is four fly stitches to the left, then four to the right. A quintuple featherstitch has five fly stitches to the left, then five to the right. So on and sew forth (10.14b).

10.14b

10.14a

10.15a

Let's work a single featherstitch. Forget about your bellybutton for this one!

Come up at the left shoulder. Insert the needle at the right shoulder and scoop up at the left HIP, keeping the thread under the tip of the needle (straight down from the left shoulder). Bring thread through (10.15a).

10.15b

The left hip now becomes the left shoulder. Insert the needle at the right shoulder. Scoop up at the left hip, keeping the thread under the tip of needle. Bring thread through (10.15b).

10.15c

Continue. A single feather can be stitched with shoulder, shoulder, left hip. Or it can be stitched with shoulder, shoulder, right hip (10.15c)

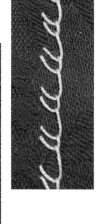

10.16a

10.16b

Double Single Feather

A double single feather is made by working a single featherstitch (shoulder, shoulder, hip), then working another single, dropping down only slightly for the shoulder and the hip. For the next stitch, drop down, leaving a bigger gap, then do two more single featherstitches placed closely together (10.16a).

Drunken Feather

I named this stitch a drunken feather because it looks like it has had one too many mimosas at Sunday brunch. The rhythm is shoulder, shoulder, left hip; shoulder, shoulder, right hip; shoulder, shoulder, left hip; shoulder, shoulder, right hip; ad infinitum (10.16b).

Maidenhair Stitch

Maidenhair can be stitched on one side or it can alternate sides (10.17).

Stitch shoulder, shoulder, left hip (10.18a). (See how all this is making sense now?!)

For the next stitch, keep the shoulders in a straight line and the hips in a straight line. The hip is now the left shoulder. Go to the right shoulder, which is even with the previous right shoulder and a little to the right. Insert the needle and come up at the new hip, which is down a little from the previous hip. Pull through (10.18b).

Once more, keeping the shoulders and hips straight, the left hip is now the left shoulder. Insert the needle at the right shoulder, which is even with the previous shoulders and a little to the right. Insert the needle and come up at the new hip, which is down a little from the previous hip. Pull through (10.18c).

To start the next set of stitches, the hip is now a left shoulder. Insert the needle at the right shoulder, scoop up at the left hip. Pull through (10.18d).

To make the next stitch, the left hip is now the left shoulder. Go to the right shoulder (even with previous shoulder) and scoop up at the left hip (down a little from previous hip). Pull through (10.18e).

To make the next stitch, the left hip is now the left shoulder. Go to the right shoulder (even with the previous shoulder) and scoop up at the left hip (down a little from the previous hip). Pull through (10.18f).

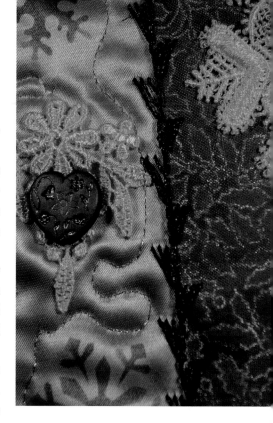

10.17

10.18a

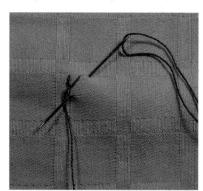

10.18b

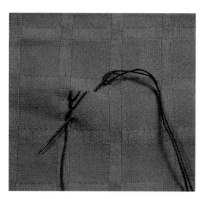

10.18c

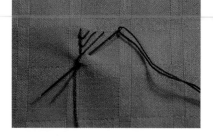

10.18d

10.18e

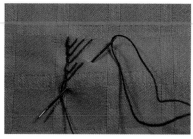

10.18f

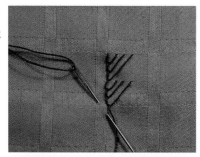

10.19a

10.19b

10.19c

As I stated earlier, maidenhair stitch can also alternate sides. Start by making the first three stitches of maidenhair as above. To swing to the left, the hip is now the right shoulder. Insert the needle at the left shoulder and scoop up at the right hip. Pull through (10.19a).

To make the next stitch, the hip is now the right shoulder. Insert the needle at the left shoulder, and scoop up at the right hip (down a little from the previous hip). Pull through (10.19b).

To make the next stitch, the hip is now the right shoulder. Insert the needle at the left shoulder, and scoop up at the right hip (down a little from the previous hip). Pull through (10.19c).

Continue alternating left and right along the seam.

10.20a

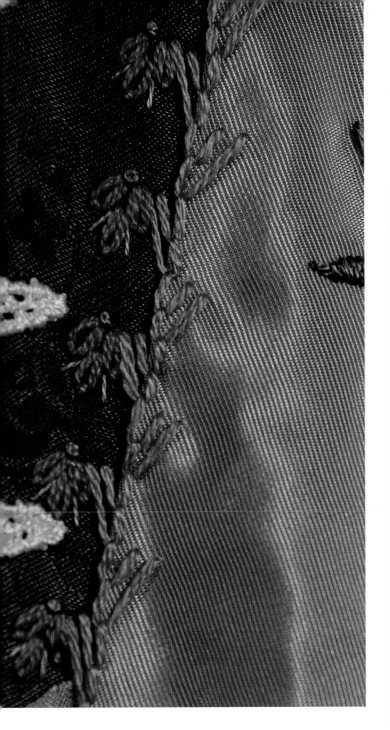

10.20b

10.20c

Raining Feathers

I first saw this stitch on an antique crazy quilt and fell in love with its free-form nature (10.21a). I flip the work upside down so the shoulders are at the bottom of the piece. I stitch randomly—perhaps three stitches to the left, two to the right, one to the left, then four to the right. Go to the next stitch and randomly stitch again. A variegated thread looks terrific used this way (10.21b).

10.21a

10.21b

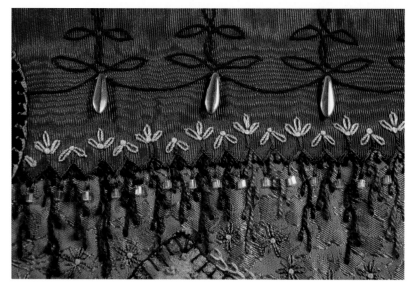

Bushes

If you take the idea of raining feathers, then turn it upside down (right side up?) and add layers of colors and threads, you can make some very interesting bushes (10.22a). I like to start and stop in various places to give the idea of growth. Think organically here. Notice the raining featherstitch above the paisley motif in figure 10.22b. The shoulders are not straight across. Think of *The Hunchback of Notre Dame* as you stitch these.

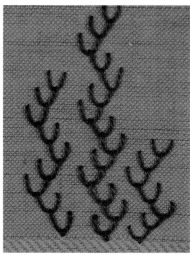

10.22a

10.22b

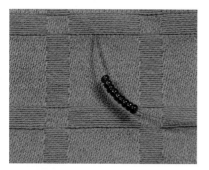

10.23a

10.23b

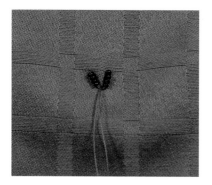

10.23c

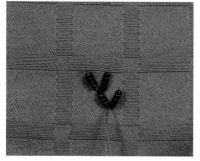

10.23d

Beaded Feather

You can easily create featherstitches with beads. You can use seed beads, bugle beads, and larger beads. The rhythm is the same as regular feather-stitch. Instead of embroidery thread, you will use a double strand of sewing thread in a quilter's #10 needle.

Come up at the left shoulder and bring thread through. String on eight seed beads (10.23a).

Insert the needle at the right shoulder and scoop up at the bellybutton, keeping the thread under the tip of the needle, but also making sure four beads go to the left and four go to the right (10.23b).

Pull thread through (10.23c).

String on eight more beads. Insert the needle at the right shoulder, scoop up at the bellybutton, keeping the thread under the tip of the needle, but also making sure four beads go to the left and four go to the right. Pull thread through (10.23d).

Continue.

To create the two colors of beaded feather, come up at the left shoulder and string on one pearl, six seed beads, and one pearl. Insert your needle at the right shoulder and place a pearl and three seed beads on the left side and three seed beads and one pearl on the other. You need to string them on in a mirror image if they are to line up properly as you stitch (10.24b).

10.24b

To place the bugle beads, come up at the left shoulder and string on two bugle beads. Insert the needle at the right shoulder, then place a bugle bead on the left side and a bugle bead on the right side (10.24c).

Figure 10.25 shows some more examples of how you can play with featherstitches: raining feathers in a very regimented way; featherstitch with nine feathers in each direction; a curvy featherstitch line; mirrored quintuple featherstitch; rows of featherstitches tightly packed together; featherstitch heart; and featherstitch circles.

10.25

Chain Stitch & Variations

HAIN STITCH is another useful, versatile stitch. A single chain stitch is a lazy daisy. A line of lazy daisies is chain stitch. You can do many things with chain stitch: whip it, decorate it, make it magic, bullion-tip it, cable chain, and make it the head of a bull.

Bring the needle up. Notice how I have placed the working thread as I pulled it through the fabric, in a loop toward the top, circling to the right (11.1a).

Insert the needle just to the right of where the thread is emerging. Take a scoop of the fabric, keeping the thread under the tip of the needle (11.1b).

Pull the thread through. Don't pull too tightly on the thread if you want your lazy daisy to be nice and fat. The more firmly you tug on the thread as you come through, the narrower the lazy daisy (11.1c).

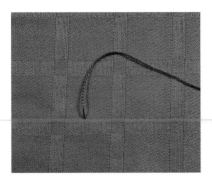

11.1a

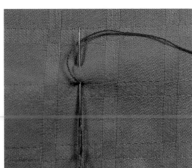

11.1b

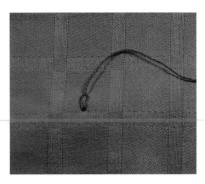

11.1c

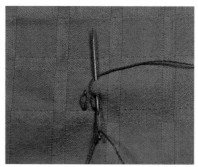

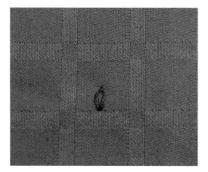

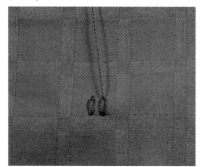

Plunge the needle down through the fabric beyond the edge of the lazy daisy. You can take a short tie-down stitch or a longer tie-down stitch. A lone stitch like this is a lazy daisy (11.1d). A chain stitch is a chain of lazy daisies.

Make the lazy daisy as above. However, instead of taking the tie-down stitch, make another chain.

Insert the needle inside the first lazy daisy just to the right of where the thread is emerging from the fabric (11.1e). Take a scoop of the fabric, keeping the thread under the tip of the needle (11.1f).

Continue with the chain (11.1g).

In figure 11.2, a lazy daisy is added to the closed blanket stitch on the right. Straight stitches are added on either side. To create the lazy-daisy seam beneath the herringbone seam, I first stitched a long lazy daisy at the end of each light blue herringbone stitch. Then, instead of tying the stitch down, I added one lazy daisy going to the left and another going to the right.

11.2

This silk dupioni fabric is woven with little squares. To embellish the fabric a bit, I stitched lazy daisies at each intersection. French knots were added in the center (11.3a). Rose montees were stitched in the alternating intersections (11.3b).

Sometimes, a seam treatment isn't even on a seam, but, rather, meanders in the middle of a fabric. The glass flower bead was sewn down. Lazy daisies form radiating petals, interspersed with green silk-ribbon straight stitches (11.4).

11.3b

11.4

11.5a

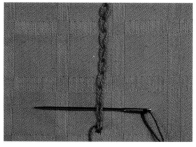

11.5b

11.5c

Whipped-Chain Stitch

Whip it good. C'mon, you had to expect that! Make a row of chain stitches in one color. Thread up with a contrasting color and bring the thread up at the bottom of the chain, just to the left of the base of the first chain. Insert the needle under the loops of the first chain stitch, just going under the loops and NOT into the fabric. Pull through (11.5a).

Continue to whip the thread under each set of loops. Always insert the needle from right to left and do NOT go through the fabric. Pull through after each stitch (11.5b).

In figure 11.5c, you can see the completed line of whipped chain.

Figure 11.6 shows whipped-chain stitches with lazy daisies at the intersections. Beads were added at the bottom.

11.6

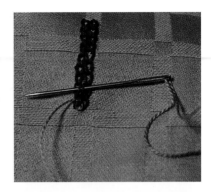

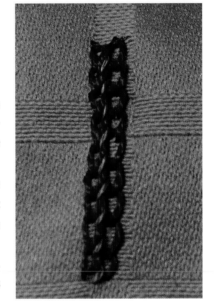

11.7a (left)
11.7b (center)
11.7c (right)

Double-Whipped Chain

To begin stitching a double-whipped chain, work two rows of chain stitches so close to one another that the chains just touch. Thread up with a contrasting color and bring up the needle at the bottom middle of the row (11.7a).

Start to whip as you did with the whipped-chain stitch, but this time you will go under the left side chain of the far right stitch and the right side chain on the left stitch. In other words, you will scoop under the two middle chains. Pull through (11.7b).

Continue catching the middle portion of the chains all the way up. Make sure you bring the needle all the way through and the tension is smooth and taut (11.7c).

Figure 11.7d shows a completed double-whipped chain.

Figure 11.7e shows a completed double-whipped chain stitched in green running horizontally.

11.7d (above)
11.7e (below)

Decorated Lazy Daisy

Make a lazy daisy, or make four (11.8a). Thread your needle with a contrasting thread. Make a straight stitch in the open space of the lazy daisy (11.8b). Note that this thread will be completely on the inside of the lazy

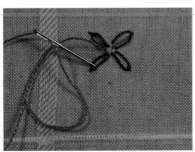

11.8a (left)
11.8b (right)

daisy. Figure 11.8c shows a seam of tied herringbone with three decorated lazy daisies on the top of the seam, extending onto the pink fabric.

This seam is a stem-stitch alternating curve with straight stitches making up the spokes of the half-wheel and green stem stitches for the stems (11.8d). Decorated lazy daisies form the floral buds on the stem. I also added French knots (11.8e).

11.8d

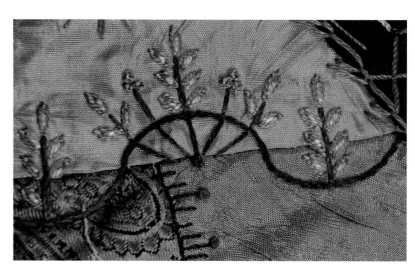

11.8e

Magic Chain!

This stitch is fun because, once you know the trick, it is easy to do, yet people are always impressed and imagine it to be much more difficult.

Start with two contrasting threads in the needle at the same time. Commence as though you are doing a lazy daisy (11.9a).

Decide which color you want for the first chain. Make sure that the thread stays under the tip of the needle. The other color thread will not go under the tip of the needle (11.9b).

11.9a

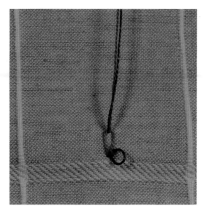

11.9b

11.9c

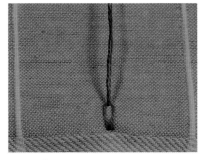

11.9d

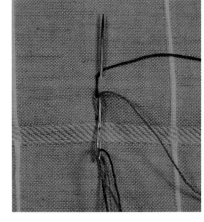

11.9e

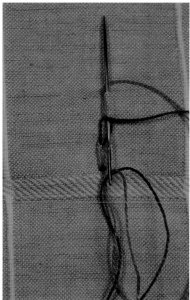

11.10a

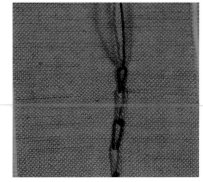

11.10b

When you pull the needle through, the color that was under the tip formed the chain. The other thread was pulled through. Sometimes, the other colored thread won't pull all the way through. This is not a problem; gently tug that thread (blue in this case) at the tip of the lazy daisy and pull the thread through (11.9c).

In figure 11.9d, the threads are pulled completely through. Check the threads in the needle and make sure they are of even length. Adjust the lengths if necessary. Note the single red chain stitch.

Form the next chain as you did the first, but keep the alternate color under the tip of the needle this time. It will be a blue chain stitch. Pull the threads through. Check the thread lengths and adjust if necessary (11.9e).

Continue forming chain stitches, alternating colors (11.10a).

Completed magic chain! (11.10b)

11.10C

Everyone will guess at how this was done (11.10c). Did you go through and stitch with one color and then go back with the alternating color?? "No, it's magic!"

In figure 11.11, the fans were stitched with magic chain. Straight stitches were added afterwards. Raining feathers can also be seen in the seam treatment to the right. A painted flower girl adds a touch of whimsy.

11.11

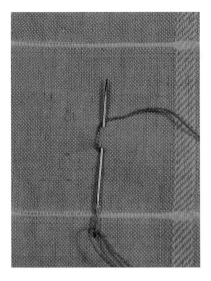 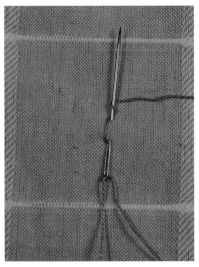 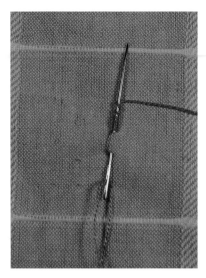

11.12a *11.12b* *11.12c*

Bullion-Tipped Lazy Daisy

Start as though you were making a lazy daisy. However, leave the needle in the fabric. DO NOT PULL THE NEEDLE THROUGH YET (11.12a).

Bring the thread that is under the needle tip around the needle and back under the tip of the needle (11.12b).

Wrap the thread three or four more times (11.12c).

Bring the tip of the needle up off the fabric and put your left index finger behind the needle (11.12d).

Bring your left thumb down, grasping the needle between thumb and index finger. Hold firmly, but not in a death choke (11.12e).

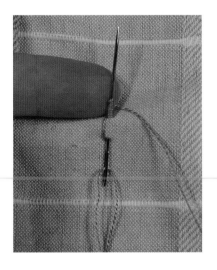 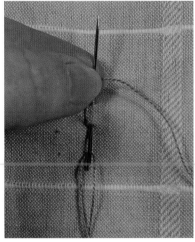

11.12d (left)
11.12e (right)

11.13a (right)
11.13b (far right)

 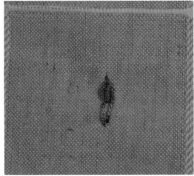

11.14a

Without letting go of the threads with your left fingers, grasp the needle with your right hand and gently pull it through. Your left hand helps the coils of thread stay in place and not spring out like a slinky gone bad (11.13a).

Pull the thread completely through and plunge the needle down into the fabric a small distance away from the end of the lazy daisy. Let the coils extend to their full length (11.13b).

Decorated lazy daisies embellish the right-hand side of the feather-stitch. Blue silk-ribbon, bullion-tipped lazy daisies form a portion of the floral bouquet in the center of the photo (11.14a).

Bullion-tipped lazy daisies sit atop a chevron/Cretan-stitch combination. Yellow herringbone stitching is below the seam. "Solace" is embroidered with stem stitch (11.14b).

11.14b

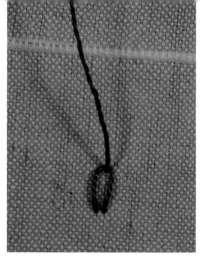

11.15a

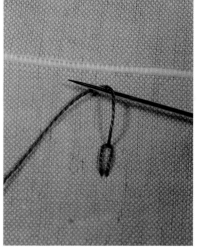

11.15b

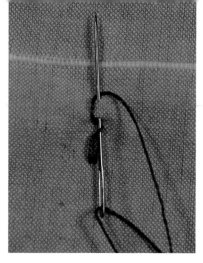

11.15c

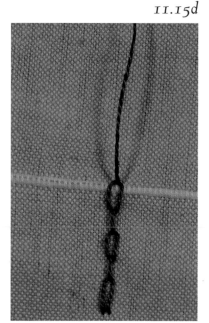

11.15d

Cable Chain

This is a nice stitch that actually looks like a chain necklace.

Start by stitching a lazy daisy (11.15a).

Watch the next step carefully. You are not inserting the needle into the fabric yet. Bring the thread around the needle as shown (11.15b).

Leave a small gap from the end of the lazy daisy before inserting the needle into the fabric to form another lazy daisy. Keep the thread under the tip of the needle. Pull through as you would when making a lazy daisy (11.15c).

The thread wrapped around the needle before inserting the needle makes that straight stitch between the lazy daisies. To form the next stitch, repeat steps two and three (11.15d).

Figure 11.16a shows cable-chain stitch worked in metallic with a glass heart bead; 11.16b shows cable chain worked in yellow silk.

11.16a

11.16b

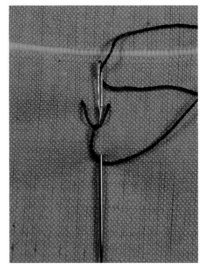

11.17a *(left)*
11.17b *(center)*
11.17c *(right)*

Tête de Boeuf Stitch (Head of the Bull)

Start by stitching a fly stitch. Do not plunge the thread to the back (11.17a).

Instead form a lazy daisy by inserting the needle just to the right of the bellybutton of the fly stitch (11.17b).

Pull through and make the tie-down stitch of the lazy daisy (11.17c). See, it sorta looks like a cow head with horns. Moooo!

Tête de Boeuf is stitched in yellow pearl cotton (11.18a) and in lavender pearl cotton (11.18b).

11.18a

11.18 b

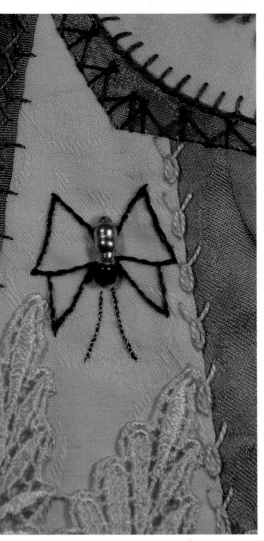

Zigzag Chain

Making a slight variation to a regular chain provides for an interesting stitch. Instead of stitching in a straight line, angle each lazy daisy of the chain stitch slightly (11.19a). The seam on the right had crystals added after the seam was stitched (11.19b).

Figure 11.19c shows a line of chain stitch. After the line of stitches were completed, extra lazy daisies were added to every other chain at forty-five-degree angles.

French Knots

DON'T KNOW how many students I have had that came into class convinced that French knots were the "F" word. Try as they might, with many a book to guide them, they had been unsuccessful at mastering this stitch. There's a good reason for that. Most books don't show enough pictures for a multi-step process. In addition, I don't know of any book that shows the importance of proper hand placement for this particular embroidery. Some people might understand the basic concept, but then twirl the needle round and round and round hoping against hope that at least one wrap will stay put as they pull their needle through the fabric.

French knots can really add a lot of dimension to an embroidered piece. They are also useful for adding just a hint of color to a bouquet or a seam treatment. French knots take on very different looks depending on which embroidery thread is used. Each of the French knots below was done with one strand and one wrap.

Figure 12.1 shows French knots worked in a variety of materials: sewing thread, silk floss, cotton floss, #12 pearl cotton, #8 pearl cotton, #5 pearl cotton, Frosty Rays, and silk ribbon.

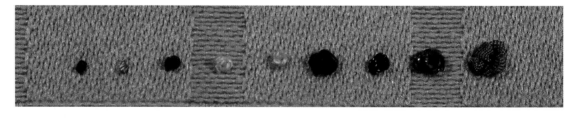

12.1

12.2

This is a block I made to raise money for Hurricane Katrina relief (12.2). The peacock on the top half of the block was influenced by a Dover Publication line drawing of a gate. It is stem stitched with a metallic braid. The body of the peacock is satin stitched. The heart motif shows French knots added to blanket stitch.

If you have tried French knots in the past and failed, fret no more. Here's how to do a one-wrap French knot so it will come out perfectly every time—even if you stitch with a strand of sewing thread!

First, position your hand and thread properly. Then bring the thread through the fabric. Place the thread over your left palm as shown (12.3a).

12.3a

Close your hand so your thumb is lightly grasping the thread. Note the thread is inside your hand (12.3b).

Some people have a tendency to grasp the thread so it is emerging at the gap between the thumb and index finger. You won't be able to make the French knot with the thread in that position. Make sure it is inside your hand as shown.

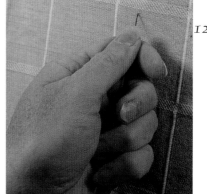

12.3b

Throughout the stitch your left hand will move the thread and your right hand will move the needle (12.3c).

12.3c

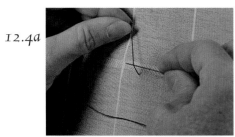

12.4a

The needle in the right hand stays still! The left hand moves the thread! Bring the thread up and above the needle (12.4a).

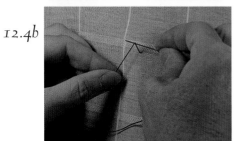

12.4b

The left hand wraps the thread behind the needle and down. Now that the thread has been wrapped, the right hand comes back into play (12.4b).

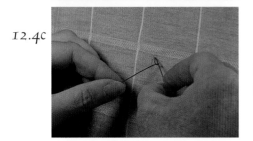

12.4c

Carefully note that the right hand has moved the tip of the needle to be inserted just to the RIGHT of where the thread is emerging from the fabric (12.4c). To do this motion, move the tip of the needle clockwise.

12.4d

Use your left hand to slightly pull the thread outward. This slides the knot down the needle so the knot is resting on the face of the fabric. This keeps a nice tight knot rather than one that looks "sproinged" (12.4d).

The needle is now inserted halfway through the fabric (12.5a). The left hand is still keeping tension on the thread so the knot stays firmly against the face of the fabric.

The right hand can let go of the needle on the top of the fabric and go beneath the fabric to grasp the needle and pull it completely through. The left hand will continue to grasp the thread until the knot is nearly completely made. Then, the left hand releases the thread and the thread is pulled all the way through the fabric (12.5b).

The object of our desire! It seems like way too many steps for such a small result. However, done in this fashion, a French knot can be laundered and suffer some abuse and still keep its shape (12.5c).

12.5a (left)
12.5b (center)
12.5c (right)

As you become adept, all these steps reduce in time to just a few seconds. It's the positioning and knowing which hand does what with needle and thread that is important.

Figure 12.6 shows yellow French knots added to blue rickrack along a seam.

French knots in a variegated color scheme fill in the "holes" of the lace surrounding this gypsy print (12.7a). I added silk-ribbon roses and leaves, pearls, and beads to enhance the gypsy print. I stitched French knots in just half of the lace to keep the motif from becoming overwhelmed.

12.7a

141

12.8

This cottage print has been stitched heavily with French knots in various threads and ribbons (12.7b). I also placed loop flowers, bullion-knot roses, and lazy daisies. This could be used as the centerpiece of a crazy-quilt wall hanging. A pieced crazy-quilt border would set off the cottage print to very good effect.

Here's a tiny motif with my thumb in the photograph for reference (12.8). See how small those French knots lining the inside oval are?

Pistil Stitch

Pistil stitch is a French knot on a stalk. You will begin just as you would when making a French knot. The difference comes in where you place the needle into the fabric after you have done your wrap. Instead of putting the needle just to the right of where the thread is emerging from the fabric, go out a distance from where the thread is emerging (12.9).

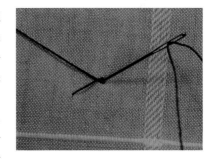

12.9

The lazy daisy flowers have purple pistil stitches between each stitch. Square beads were added in the center. Note the French knots at the bottom of the twisted herringbone seam, forming the silk ribbon forget-me-nots, and in the center of the triangle motifs (12.10a).

This seam is composed of triple featherstitching to which a triple lazy daisy has been added. I then embroidered pistil stitch between the lazy daisies. Note the French knots that I added to the row of embroidered Cretan stitch (12.10b).

12.10a

12.10b

Beads

EADS ARE lovely embellishments that allow you to add color, shape, sparkle, and texture to your embroidery. Wide varieties of beads in multiple shapes, colors, and materials are available in fabric and craft stores and from online sources. You can also find beautiful beads and pearls in pieces of vintage costume jewelry.

To secure a single bead, use a doubled length of thread, knotted. Come up through the fabric, and sew on a bead as you normally would by running your needle through the hole. Then come up through the fabric again. This time, however, instead of putting your needle through the hole in the bead, split the thread and railroad the bead, running one thread on one side of the bead and the other on the other side of the bead. Then sew through the fabric on the other side of the bead (13.1).

13.1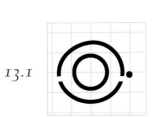

Couching Beads

You will need two needles for this technique. One needle should hold a double length of thread, knotted, for stringing the beads. The other should hold a single strand of thread, knotted, for couching. Bring the needle with the double strand of thread up through the fabric. String on four to five beads (or whatever number is required). Do not sew down through the fabric. Then bring the needle with the single strand up through the fabric and "staple" (stitch) the double length of thread down. String on a few more beads, staple, and repeat (13.2). I refer to this stitch as a staple

13.2

because your needle should not come up and go down in the same exact hole. Doing that would make the line of beads buckle. If you go over just a few threads from where the couching thread emerges, then plunge down over the double length, you will get a much more satisfactory result.

Backstitching Beads

To backstitch beads, use a double length of thread, knotted. String on five beads, then sew down through the fabric. Bring your needle up through the fabric between the third and fourth beads. Sew through the holes of beads four and five. String on three more beads and sew down through the fabric. Bring your needle up to the left of the second bead you have just strung. Go through the holes of the last two beads strung (13.3). String on three more beads. Repeat.

A beaded snowflake, beaded featherstitch, and a beaded bugle-bead/seed-bead seam make this winter crazy-quilt block come to life (13.5a). The green seed beads placed on the green lace add depth and contrast (13.5b). The lace motif in figure 13.5c has been enhanced with jewel-toned seed beads.

13.3

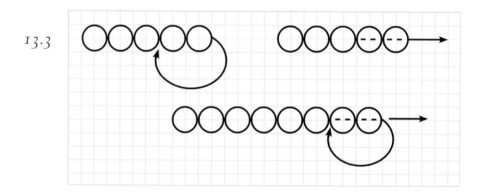

13.4

13.5a

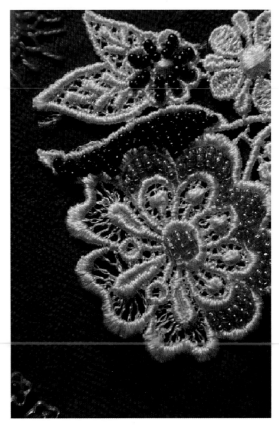
13.5b (left)

13.5c (right)

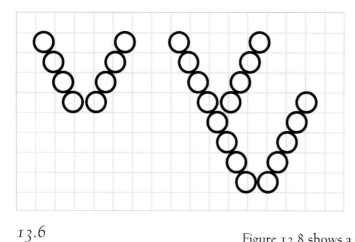

13.6

To featherstitch with beads, use a double length of thread, knotted. Bring your needle up through the fabric at the left shoulder, then string on eight beads. Make a featherstitch by inserting your needle at the right shoulder and scooping up at the bellybutton. Make sure four beads go on one side and four beads go on the other side. Then string on eight more beads and featherstitch (13.6). Be sure that your hand always stays on top of the fabric for this stitch.

Figure 13.8 shows a variation of featherstitch with two bugle beads.

13.7a

13.7b

13.8

This variation combines bugle and seed beads (13.9). String the beads in this order: seed, bugle, bugle, seed (13.10).

To blanket stitch with beads, use a double length of thread, knotted. Bring your needle up through the fabric, then string on eight beads. Make a blanket stitch by advancing to the right and taking a stitch from the bottom to the top, keeping the thread under the tip of the needle. Make sure four beads go on top and four beads go to the right. String on eight more beads; blanket stitch (13.11). Continue.

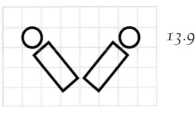

13.9

13.10

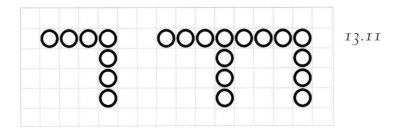

13.11

Figures 13.12a and b show a variation: blanket stitch with two bugle beads. Combine bugle and seed beads, stringing bugle, seed, then bugle.

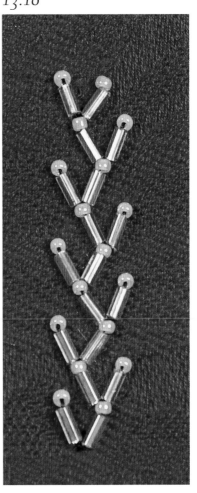

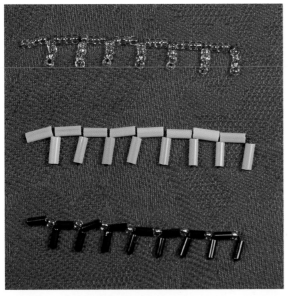
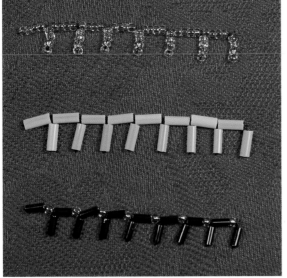

13.12a

13.12b

13.13

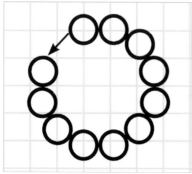

13.14

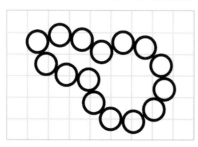

13.15

Beaded stars are fun to sprinkle across a patch, to stitch on a seam line, or add to a motif. These are worked in your hand and then sewn down to the fabric when each star is completed (13.13).

To create stars, cut a 2' length of beading thread. String on ten seed beads. Leaving a 6" tail, tie the beads into a circle. Make sure your knots are very secure! Pass the needle through the first bead in the circle (13.14).

String on five beads. Skip the next bead in the circle. Pass your needle through the next bead in the circle (13.15).

Continue around until you have five star arms. Knot the thread. Weave in tails of thread, then end off (13.16).

Figure 13.17 shows two variations of beaded stars.

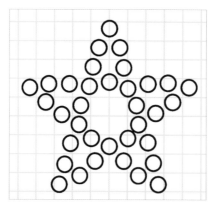

13.16

13.17

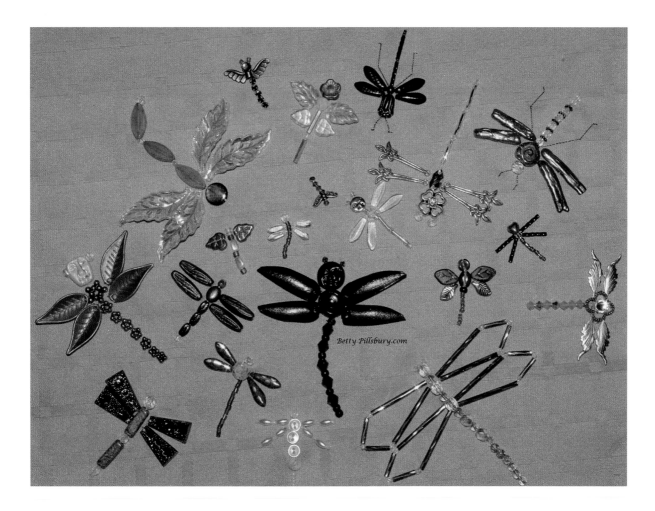

Dragonfly Beaded Motif

These directions are for the large motif in the center of the picture (13.18). Once you have an idea of how to make a dragonfly, look through your bead stash and find other beads to make them!!

Supplies:
  13 mm glass-face bead
  13 mm spiral-disc bead
  Seven round beads, size 8
  Five bicone beads, size 6 mm
  Two bicone beads, size 3 mm
  Four beetle wings
  Sewing needle and sewing thread

Using a doubled, knotted sewing thread in a sewing needle, string on the glass-face bead, the spiral-disc bead and the alternating round and 6 mm bicone beads as shown in figure 13.18. Notice there are two rounds at the end of the dragonfly tail. End off the thread with a secure knot.

Using a single strand of sewing thread in a sewing needle, couch the dragonfly tail in a pleasing manner. Couch between the face bead and spiral-disc bead. End off the thread with a secure knot.

Using a doubled, knotted sewing thread in a sewing needle, sew on the beetle wings as shown. End off the thread with a secure knot.

Using a doubled, knotted sewing thread in a sewing needle, sew on the 3mm bicone beads next to the face bead as shown in the picture.

13.19

Pearl Flower

Materials:
Green cotton floss
4 mm bead cap
4 mm oat beads
4 mm crystals
3 mm round bead
Green seed beads, size 11

On tissue paper, trace the stem only (13.20). Baste the tissue paper onto the seam line. Stem stitch with two strands floss. (I used DMC 936.) Remove the basting stitches and the tissue paper. Create beaded flowers by stitching through a bead cap (13.21a), a round bead, and a bead cap for the flower's center (13.21b). Sew six crystals around the center as in figure 13.19. Sew oat beads between crystals. Using seed beads, lazy daisy the leaves.

13.20

13.21a (left)
13.21b (right)

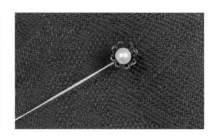

Bead Flower and Ribbon Seam

Materials:

7 mm silk ribbon
Lucite baby's breath beads
Seed beads
Bugle beads, size 2 (6 mm)
#8 pearl cotton

Trace dotted straight lines onto tissue paper (13.23). The long solid line is the seam line and is used for placement only. Baste the tissue paper onto the fabric, matching the seam line. Using #8 pearl cotton, stitch the straight dotted lines, securely knotting off after each stitch. Using 7 mm silk ribbon and a chenille needle, tread the silk ribbon under and over the straight stitches as shown in figure 13.22. Sew on bugle beads. Sew a Lucite flower placing a crystal silver-lined seed bead as its center. Add crystal silver-lined seed beads on the silk ribbon as shown.

13.23

Mini Rickrack Beaded Fringe

Materials:
Mini velvet rickrack
6 mm heart beads
10 x 9 mm heart beads
21 x 7 mm metal wing beads
4 mm crystals
Clear silver-lined seed beads

Sew mini rickrack along the seam line. Create fringe from each downward point of the rickrack as follows:

String three seed beads, small heart, one seed bead; come back through the strung beads and plunge the needle down through the point of rickrack and through the fabric. Come up at the next point of rickrack.

String six seed beads, small heart, one seed bead; come back through the strung beads and plunge the needle down through the point of rickrack and through the fabric. Come up at the next point of rickrack.

*String two seed beads, one crystal, two seed beads, one crystal, two seed beads, wings, heart, three seed beads; come back through the strung beads and plunge the needle down through the point of rickrack and through the fabric. Come up at the next point of rickrack.

String six seed beads, small heart, one seed bead; come back through the strung beads and plunge the needle down through the point of rickrack and through the fabric. Come up at next the point of rickrack.

String three seed beads, small heart, one seed bead; come back through the strung beads and plunge the needle down through the point of rickrack and through the fabric. Come up at the next point of rickrack.

String six seed beads, small heart, one seed bead; come back through the strung beads and plunge the needle down through the point of rickrack and through the fabric. Come up at the next point of rickrack.

Continue from * across.

Beaded Fringe

Materials:

Gimp braid
Seed beads
4 mm crystals
Dagger beads

Using tacking stitches, sew the gimp braid to the fabric. Bring up a double strand of sewing thread to the left edge of the gimp braid, about ¼"
from the edge. Bring needle out at loop on gimp. String ten seed beads, a
4 mm crystal, and ten seed beads. Skip four loops, stitch through the left
side of the next loop. Come back up through the center of the same loop.
String five seed beads, a 4 mm crystal, a seed bead, and a dagger bead. Go
back through the just-strung seed bead, the 4 mm crystal and five seed
beads, then stitch through the center of the loop. Come back up through
the right side of the same loop. String ten seed beads, a 4 mm crystal, and
ten seed beads. Skip four loops, stitch through the left side of the next
loop. Come back up through the center of the same loop. String three
seed beads, a 4 mm crystal, five seed beads, a 4 mm crystal, a seed bead,
and a dagger bead. Go back through the last-strung seed bead only. String
a 4 mm crystal and five seed beads. Go back through the first 4 mm crystal and three seed beads. Stitch through the center of the loop. Continue
stitching following the diagram in figure 13.26.

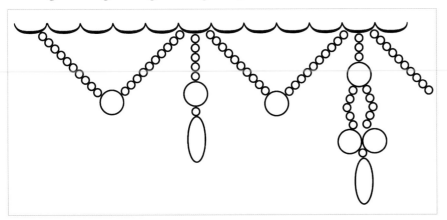

Beaded Picot Lace

Condition 3' of beading thread and thread into a beading needle. Leaving a 6" tail thread, put on a stop bead. (A stop bead is a bead used to keep the working beads from sliding off; you will remove it later. Simply go through the bead hole twice.) String on six beads and push them all the way down to the stop bead. Go through the next to the last bead you just strung. You just made a picot. Make sure the tension is taut.

String on three beads. Skip three beads from the picot and go through the next bead.

String on three beads. Go through the next to the last bead you just strung (another picot).

String on three beads. Go through the middle bead of the set of three.

Repeat steps three and four, going back and forth until your lace is the desired length.

To end off the working thread, knot off between two beads, string through a few more beads and knot off between two beads again, string through a few more beads and cut the thread (13.28).

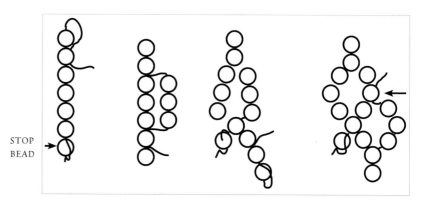

Pearl Seam Treatment

Materials:

Tissue paper
4 mm round pearls
4 mm rice (oat) pearls
Sewing needle and sewing thread

Trace the curlicue pattern onto your fabric (13.30a). If your fabric is dark, trace the design onto tissue paper. Baste the tissue paper onto the fabric. Using the 2.5 mm pearls, stitch the curlicue, leaving a space between the pearls. Add six pearls to the inside curve of the curlicue, as shown in figure 13.29. Add the oval pearls, as shown. Remember to railroad those pearls!

A similar curlicue (13.30b) can be stitched in silk ribbon with French knots (13.31).

13.29

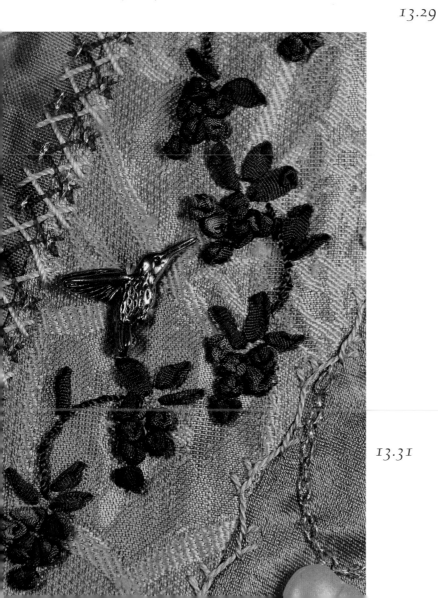

13.31

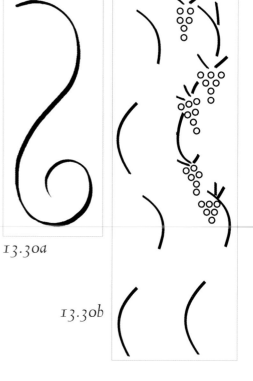

13.30a

13.30b

14

Fabulous Flowers

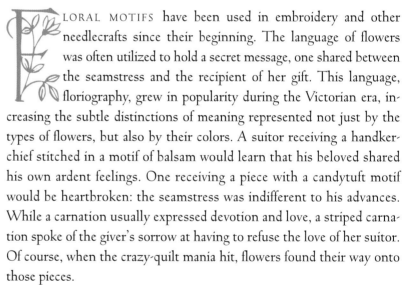

14.1b

14.1c

FLORAL MOTIFS have been used in embroidery and other needlecrafts since their beginning. The language of flowers was often utilized to hold a secret message, one shared between the seamstress and the recipient of her gift. This language, floriography, grew in popularity during the Victorian era, increasing the subtle distinctions of meaning represented not just by the types of flowers, but also by their colors. A suitor receiving a handkerchief stitched in a motif of balsam would learn that his beloved shared his own ardent feelings. One receiving a piece with a candytuft motif would be heartbroken: the seamstress was indifferent to his advances. While a carnation usually expressed devotion and love, a striped carnation spoke of the giver's sorrow at having to refuse the love of her suitor. Of course, when the crazy-quilt mania hit, flowers found their way onto those pieces.

Gathered Flower

This technique can achieve a number of different effects, depending on your choice of ribbon. Figure 14.1 shows gathered flowers made from silk bias ribbon (a), a glitter-edged rayon (b), and a wired-edge rayon (c).

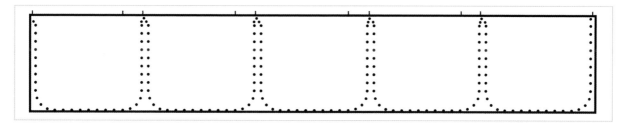

Cut a 6" length of ⅞" wired-rayon ribbon. Thread a sewing needle with a doubled length of sewing thread and knot the ends. Starting ½" from the cut edge, sew through the ribbon, close to the selvage. Take another stitch in the same place to anchor the knot. Now, work a running stitch along the path shown (14.2). The dots represent the path, but do not show how close the stitches should be! Each petal is 1" wide. End ½" from the cut edge.

Gently gather the ribbon up. Take the needle through the ribbon close to where the original knot started. Take another stitch to anchor the thread. Knot off and clip the thread (14.3).

14.2

14.3

Velvet Rickrack Flower

Cut a 5" length of ⅝" velvet rickrack. Thread a sewing needle with a double length of knotted thread. Work through the points of the rickrack on one side as shown (14.4). Gather tightly. Knot the thread on back and cut the thread.

Sew a pearl to the center of the flower, if desired (14.5).

Cut a 6" length of ⅝" velvet ribbon. Thread a sewing needle with a double length of knotted thread. Secure the thread ⅛" from the cut edge,

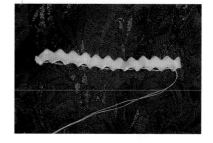

14.4

14.5

along the selvage. Run a basting stitch along one long side, as shown (14.6).

Gather tightly. Turn back the cut edges slightly and sew. Secure the thread and end off. Sew a pearl in the center, if desired.

Gather tightly. Turn back the cut edges slightly and sew. Secure the thread and end off. Sew a pearl in the center, if desired.

Velvet Yo-yo Flower

Using a circle template, trace a circle on the wrong side of the velvet. Cut the circle from the fabric. Thread a sewing needle with a double length of knotted thread. Turn under one edge of the fabric by ⅛" and run a basting stitch around, through the doubled-over edge. Gather tightly. Knot off and end the thread. When you sew the yo-yo down, add beads along the edge (14.5), in the center (14.7), or wherever strikes your fancy (14.8)!

14.8

14.7

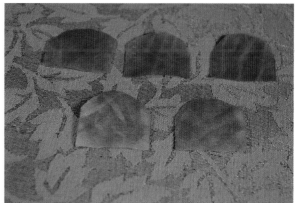

14.9 (left)

14.10 (right)

Country Rose

Materials:

Sewing, embroidery, and chenille needles
Sewing thread
Fray Check
Empty baggie on which to put a puddle of Fray Check
Water-soluble pen
Five inches of 32 mm silk ribbon for each Country Rose flower
Small amount of yellow pearl cotton

14.11

Cut five 1" pieces of the 32 mm silk ribbon. Trim the upper edges of the ribbon as shown (14.10). Basically, you are rounding the corners. Notice the selvage of the ribbon is on the sides and the cut edges are the top and bottom.

Squeeze a small puddle of Fray Check onto a plastic baggie. Carefully, touch the edge of the cut rounded corners through the Fray Check. Barely touch into the Fray Check. It will quickly wick into the silk ribbon! Do the same with the bottom of the petal (the other cut edge). Set petal aside to dry. Drying will take only a few minutes (14.11).

Roll the rounded corner around a chenille needle (14.12) and steam with a steam iron. Keep your fingers back!! Steam from the iron is painful!

14.12

14.13

14.14a

14.14b

14.15a

Once all five petals have been rolled and steamed, you can gather them to form a rose. Thread a sewing needle with a double length of sewing thread and knot the ends. Run a basting stitch through the long cut end of the ribbon, about ⅛" from the edge (14.13).

Do NOT knot off or end the thread. Continue to baste the bottom of the next petal. Continue until all five petals have been basted onto the length of thread (14.14a).

Bring the needle through the first petal, close to where the original knot in the sewing thread began. Gently pull the sewing thread up tightly. Sew through the ribbon again to secure the thread. Knot off the thread, but do not clip it yet (14.14b).

Sew the flower to a small square of buckram. Knot off and clip the sewing thread (14.15a).
Trim the buckram square close to the sewn line. Sew the Country Rose to the fabric of your choice.

With the yellow pearl cotton in a crewel needle, stitch pistil stitches around the center of the rose as shown (14.15b).
For the center, you can use yellow chenille thread, more pearl cotton, beads, or a button. Add leaves as desired.

14.15b

Heart with Rolled Roses

Materials:

2 yards of ½" rayon seam binding for rolled roses
4 mm silk ribbon for leaves
Burgundy embroidery floss
#4 Kreinik braid in gold

Trace pattern onto fabric (14.17).

Stitch heart outline with two strands of embroidery floss, pearl cotton, or another embroidery thread in chain stitch. With a contrasting thread (I like to use metallic), whip the chain stitch.

Make rolled roses and add to heart.

Materials for Rolled Roses:

1 to 1½ yards of 1" double-faced satin ribbon
Sewing needle and thread
Fabric on which to place rose

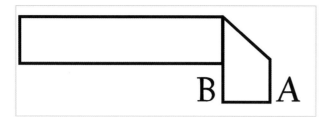

14.18

To fashion the inner part of the rose, cut an 8" length of ribbon. Starting at the right-hand side of the ribbon, measure in 2", then fold ribbon down toward you to create a forty-five-degree angle. There will be a 1" overhang (14.18).

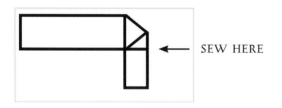

14.19

Fold the ribbon to the left so side A and side B meet. Sew tacking stitches along the bottom selvage of the ribbon. Leave the needle and thread in the ribbon and allow the needle to dangle (14.19).

With your left hand, fold the ribbon away from you to form a forty-five-degree angle.

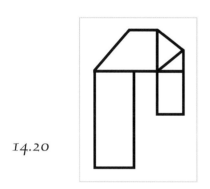

14.20

Roll the ribbon to the left, keeping the bottom selvages even (14.20). As you approach the fold, you will need to pay careful attention to keep the selvages even as you will be folding "around a corner." Take more tacking stitches. Continue folding and tacking until you reach the end of the ribbon. Securely fasten off the thread.

Add silk ribbon leaves in straight stitches (14.21).

14.21

14.22a (far left)
14.22b (left)

14.23a

Dupioni Rose

Materials:

Silk dupioni fabric, cut 2" x 18"
Sewing needle and sewing thread

14.23b

Cut a strip of dupioni silk 2" x 18". Thread a sewing needle with a matching sewing thread. Knot the end.

Tie a soft knot at one end of the silk (14.22a). Pin onto the fabric (14.22b).

Lightly twist the strip of silk and coil it around the center knot (14.23a). Pin in place (14.23b).

Continue twisting, coiling and pinning until you reach the end of the strip (14.23c).

Tuck the raw end of the strip under a petal. Tack everything in place (14.24a). Don't take so many tacking stitches that you lose the fluffiness of the rose! Remove pins. Add leaves of your choice (14.24b).

14.23c

14.24a

14.24b

14.25

Folded-Circle Flower

Materials:

Silk Essence fabric, or another non-raveling fabric
Sewing needle and sewing thread

Trace circles (14.26) onto a lightweight fabric that does not ravel easily. Silk Essence is a great fabric for this. It is a polyester that gathers easily and won't ravel like a silk dupioni.

Fold each fabric circle in half, and then again in quarters (14.27a). You will see that on one side of the fabric you have a double fold. Always start the gathering from the double fold.

With a doubled sewing thread that is knotted, gather along the side of the circle, about ⅛" in from the cut edge (14.27b).

14.26

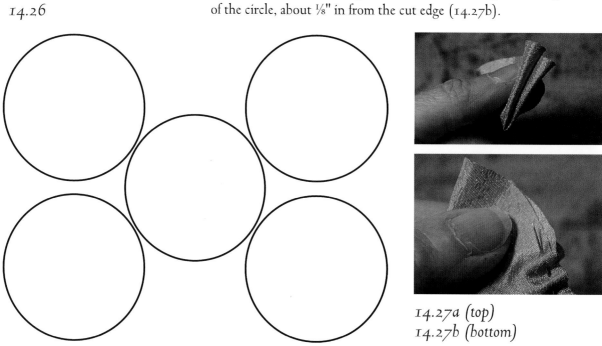

14.27a *(top)*
14.27b *(bottom)*

When you finish gathering one petal, do NOT end off the thread. Fold the next circle in half and then quarters and start gathering from the double-fold edge as before (14.28).

Continue to add more petals until you have enough for the flower you have in mind.

If you make four petals, it rather looks like a dogwood blossom. You can do seven petals, as shown on the flower at far right. A button center and beaded dragonfly has been added. The center flower has a similar base of seven petals. Then, another layer of seven petals were added on top. You can make this layer with slightly smaller circles, or with circles of the same size.

Make your flowers in a burgundy color and they will look like poinsettias. In yellow, they will look like sunflowers. In figure 14.29, the full flower and buds have been added around a cabochon.

14.28

14.29

167

14.30

Fantasy Flower

Materials:

3 yards 7 mm silk ribbon for outer petals
3 yards 7 mm silk ribbon for outer bit of the center
3 yards of 4 mm silk ribbon for center
3 yards of 4 mm silk ribbon for outer petals
Pearl cotton to match the outer bit of the center

Trace pattern (14.31) onto fabric.

Using 4 mm silk ribbon in a chenille needle, fill the center circle with French knots (14.32).

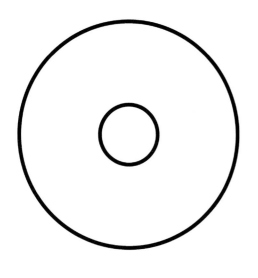

14.31

14.32

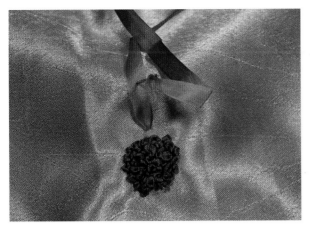

14.33ᵃ

14.33ᵇ

14.34

Leaving a gap of about ⅛" and using a 7 mm silk ribbon in the chenille needle (14.33a), stitch Japanese ribbon stitches around (14.33b).

Using a 4 mm silk ribbon in the chenille needle, stitch twisted straight stitches randomly over the 7 mm stitches (14.34).

Using a 7 mm silk ribbon in the chenille needle, stitch Fargo roses in the gap between the French knots. Start by wrapping the silk ribbon around the needle as though you were making a French knot. Then, take the tip of the needle and weave through the middle of the ribbon from the wrap to where the silk ribbon is coming out of the fabric (14.35a).

Plunge the needle through the fabric next to, but not in the same hole as, the place where the silk ribbon is coming out of the fabric. Draw the ribbon through slowly (14.35b).

Continue adding Fargo roses around.

14.35ᵃ (left)
14.35ᵇ (below)

14.36

With pearl cotton, add pistil stitches. (Remember, a pistil stitch is like a French knot on a stalk.) Instead of inserting the needle very close to where the thread is coming up out of the fabric, insert the needle a length away, while still keeping tension on the wrapped thread. Figure 14.36 shows the completed fantasy flower.

Varieties of flowers can be mixed on a single quilt to create a gorgeous garden, or a single variety may be placed, with perhaps the choice of bloom containing a secret message of its own. The choice and the story it tells are yours.

THANK YOU for going crazy with me. The process of crazy quilting is ever evolving, ever learning, and ever pleasurable. Take classes from as many people as you can. Peruse antique and modern crazy quilts for ideas and inspiration. Take a class in a related discipline to further your artistic toolbox. Always scan your environment for ideas.

Play with velvets and satins and beads and threads. Not only is crazy quilting a great way to express yourself, it is terrific therapy.

Wishing you best stitches,
Betty

GLOSSARY

Antique blanket stitch: My term for the stitch that looks like a blanket stitch alternating above and below the seam line.

Appliqué: Sewing a patch of fabric on top of another fabric.

Audition: When I am not sure of a fabric or embellishment, I place the item temporarily on the piece to see if the color/shape/placement works in the overall scheme.

Backstitch: Bringing thread up beyond the line of stitching and stitching back to the previous stitch.

Batting: A middle layer of material—cotton, acrylic, wool, or silk—placed to give the entire quilt loft and warmth. Batting is found in most quilts, but not necessarily in crazy quilts.

Beading: Beads added to a piece.

Blackwork: A medieval technique using black thread on a counted ground cloth.

Blanket stitch: An embroidery stitch generally used to secure and decorate the edge of a blanket.

Bobbin lace: Lace made using threads wound on bobbins.

Bullion knots: An embroidery stitch that creates a long knotted stitch reminiscent of bullion gold embroidery.

Bushes: Embroidered featherstitches grouped closely together to create the look of bushes.

Cast-on stitch: A Brazilian embroidery technique where the thread is cast on the embroidery needle in the same way as knitting stitches are cast on.

Chain stitch: An embroidery stitch resulting in a line of chains.

Chevron stitch: An embroidery stitch that resembles a V with a bar across the point.

Closed blanket stitch: A variation of a blanket stitch where the "fingers" of the stitch are not open. It resembles a triangle.

Couching: Using one thread to hold down another thread.

Counted thread: An embroidery technique where the ground fabric threads are counted to keep track of where the needle enters or exits the fabric.

Cretan stitch: An embroidery stitch that originated in Crete, often used to embellish clothing.

Crochet: A handicraft in which yarn or thread is made up into a patterned fabric by looping the yarn or thread with a hooked needle.

Cross stitch: An embroidery technique using thread to make Xs.

Crumb quilt: A quilt that utilizes small pieces of fabric in a haphazard fashion. Crumb quilts, unlike crazy quilts, are not embellished.

Cut-thread (or cutwork) embroidery: An embroidery technique where the backing fabric is cut away once the embroidery stitches are completed.

Drawn thread: An embroidery technique where threads from the cloth are drawn out to create a pattern.

Embellished quilt: A quilt that has decorative elements placed upon it.

Embellishment: Decorative elements created through a number of techniques, including embroidery, beading, and the placement of laces.

Fargo rose: A silk ribbon stitch resulting in a rose.

Featherstitch: An embroidery technique that looks like a line of fly stitches.

Fly stitch: An embroidery stitch that looks like a V.

French knot: A raised embroidery stitch in which the thread creates a knot.

Goldwork: An embroidery technique utilizing gold threads to create a pattern.

Hardanger embroidery: A counted and drawn thread technique, originating in the Hardanger region of Norway.

Hedebo: A style of Danish embroidery, traditionally done in white thread on white cloth, using pulled and drawn thread techniques.

Herringbone stitch: An embroidery stitch named for its resemblance to the bones along the spine of a herring.

Interlaced herringbone: A variation of herringbone in which a secondary thread laces through the foundation herringbone.

Interrupted herringbone: A variation of herringbone in which the line of stitches stops and starts.

Japanese ribbon stitch: A silk ribbon stitch in which the needle pierces the ribbon stitch.

Kensington stitch: The Victorian Kensington School of Embroidery popularized this version of the long and short stitch to create realism in embroidery.

Lazy daisy: A single chain stitch.

Mountmellick work: An Irish technique using thick white threads on a white ground fabric.

Needlepoint: Embroidery (usually counted) on a canvas ground.

Needle tatting: Tatting created using a needle rather than a shuttle.

Nook and cranny: My term for creating interest in piecing fabrics by having some pieces of fabric jut out onto another piece of fabric, rather than lining up the edges.

Or nué embroidery: Medieval embroidery using gold and silk threads to create a scene.

Outline stitch: An embroidery technique used to outline an embroidery pattern.

Picot: An embroidery or beading technique used on edges to give a regular looped edging.

Pistil stitch: A French knot on a stalk used to resemble pistils in a flower.

Pulled thread: An embroidery technique in which the threads of the ground fabric are pulled together with an embroidery thread to create patterns.

Quilting: A running stitch that goes through three layers of a traditional quilt.

Rachel thread: An embroidery thread that resembles a translucent tube.

Raining feathers: My term for a series of featherstitches worked upside down, as though they were raining down.

Redwork embroidery: An embroidery technique using red thread on a white ground fabric, usually in stem or outline stitch.

Richelieu embroidery: A French embroidery technique utilizing cut-thread and surface embroidery.

Sampler work: A demonstration of the techniques one is learning or has mastered.

Sashing: In quilting, sashing is fabric that is sewn to frame a quilt block.

Satin stitch: An embroidery technique in which threads lie side by side to create a colored-in look.

Scrap quilt: A quilt that uses many pieces of leftover fabrics.

Sew and flip: A technique used to attach two pieces of fabric. Place the two pieces right sides together, and sew along one edge. Flip the top piece over and the two pieces are now sewn together with the right sides of the fabric facing up.

Shadow chevron stitch: A variation of chevron stitch in which a secondary thread creates a shadow effect.

Shadow herringbone: A variation of herringbone stitch in which a secondary thread creates a shadow effect.

Shadow work: An embroidery technique that uses herringbone stitch on the backside of a translucent fabric to create a soft, shadow effect.

Silk ribbon: Embroidery ribbon, made of silk, in varying widths.

Split stitch: An embroidery stitch in which the current stitch pierces, or splits, the previous stitch.

Stem stitch: An embroidery stitch that provides a smooth outline of a pattern.

Straight stitch: An embroidery stitch that comes up at one point and goes straight down to another point.

Stumpwork: A historic embroidery technique using dimensional effect to give interest to a piece.

Surface embroidery: A general term for embroidery that sits on top of a ground cloth (rather than pulled or drawn stitching).

Threaded stem stitch: A variation of stem stitch in which a secondary thread is laced through the stem stitch.

Twisted herringbone: A variation of herringbone in which the needle takes an extra pass to twist the ends of the stitch.

Tying: Making a knot.

Whipped stem stitch: A variation of stem stitch in which a secondary thread is used to give contrast and interest.

Whole cloth quilt: A quilt that has not been pieced with fabric. One whole piece of material has been used as the ground.

Woven herringbone: A variation of herringbone in which a secondary thread has been used to weave in and out of the herringbone stitch.

RESOURCES

www.bettypillsbury.com
www.vintagevogue.com
www.flightsoffancyboutique.com
www.hand-dyedfibers.com
www.delectablemountain.com
www.florilegium.com
www.colourcomplements.com
www.theedwardianneedle.com
www.nordicneedle.com
www.doverpublications.com
www.mag.cloud.com/user/kitty-and-me
www.artbeads.com
www.fusionbeads.com

INDEX

Italic numbers indicate illustrations of quilts referred to by title within the text.

antique blanket stitch, 34, 73, 99, 104, 173. *See also* blanket stitch

appliqué, 23, 27, 41–44, 51, 65, 103, 173

audition, 28, 41, 42, 173

backstitch, 146, 173; illustrated instructions for, 146

batting, 23, 173

beaded feather, 122–24, 146, 148–49; illustrated instructions for, 122. *See also* featherstitch

beading, 16, 150, 156, 167, 173

beads, 22, 27, 28, 30, 31–32, 45, 46, 60, 67, 70, 72, 75, 78, 79, 82, 87, 92, 96, 98, 100, 101, 102, 104, 112, 122–24, 127, 128, 135, 141, 142, 145–57, 160, 162, 171. *See also* backstitch; blanket stitch; couching; embellishment; beaded feather; fringe; picot

Birds of a Feather, 38, 39, 40

blackwork, 16, 173

blanket stitch, 46, 65–75, 88, 99, 100, 103, 139, 149, 173; illustrated instructions for, 66, 70. *See also* antique blanket stitch; closed blanket stitch

bobbin lace, 16, 173

bullion knots, 23, 52, 143

bullion rose, 46, 69, 173

bullion-tipped lazy daisy, 73, 115, 133–34; illustrated instructions for, 133–34. *See also* chain stitch; lazy daisy

bushes, 46, 121, 173. *See also* featherstitch; raining feathers

cable chain, 135; illustrated instructions for, 135. *See also* chain stitch

cast-on stitch, 47, 173

Centennial Exposition of 1876 (Philadelphia), 5

chain stitch, 46, 63, 125–37, 163, 174; illustrated instructions for, 126. *See also* bullion-tipped lazy daisy; cable chain; double-whipped chain; lazy daisy; magic chain; tête de boeuf stitch; whipped chain; zigzag chain

chevron stitch, 45, 55, 94–98, 99, 100, 101, 103, 104, 134, 174; illustrated instructions for, 94–95. *See also* shadow chevron

choosing fabrics, 22, 36–38, 44, 48, 52–53, 57, 166

cigarette silk, 45, 46, 47, 49, 50, 92

closed blanket stitch, 74–75, 126, 174; illustrated instructions for, 74. *See also* blanket stitch

couching, 53, 96, 98, 145–46, 152, 174; illustrated instructions for, 145

counted thread, 174

crazing, 5, 7

Crazy Diamonds, 20, 21, 30–32

Crazy Patchwork and Needlework Show (Manhattan), 8, 9, 10

Crazy Work and Needle Art Show (Boston), 5, 7, 8; catalogue for, 5–7

Cretan stitch, 46–47, 87–93, 94, 99, 100–101, 102, 103, 115, 134, 143, 174; illustrated instructions for, 88

crochet, 16, 174

cross stitch, 16, 174

crumb quilt, 17, 174. *See also* scrap quilt

crystals, 46, 47, 72, 82, 100, 147, 152, 153, 154, 155. *See also* embellishment

curves, 35, 39, 41, 42, 43, 44, 46, 48, 60, 69, 78, 97, 130, 157

cut-thread embroidery, 174, 175

decorated lazy daisy, 97, 129–30, 134; illustrated instructions for, 129. *See also* lazy daisy

double-whipped chain, 129; illustrated instructions for, 129. *See also* chain stitch

Dover Publications, 23, 56, 139

dragonfly motif, 151–52

drawn thread, 16, 174. *See also* hardanger embroidery; hedebo

drunken feather, 110, 116. *See also* featherstitch

Elderberry Fairy, 17, 22

embellished quilt, 19, 174

embellishment, 18, 19, 22, 23, 37, 39, 43, 45, 46, 48, 84, 147, 173, 174. *See also* beads; crystals; fringe; lace; pearls; rickrack

embroidery, 4, 5, 7, 9, 12, 14, 16, 17, 18, 19, 20, 22, 23, 27, 28, 30, 31, 32, 34, 35, 36, 39, 45, 46, 59, 60, 61, 63, 64, 76, 87, 96, 105, 111, 122, 134, 138, 143, 145, 158, 173, 174, 175, 176; materials, 51–54; preparing for, 51–58. *See also* drawn thread; hardanger embroidery; hedebo; motifs; redwork embroidery; Richelieu embroidery; transfers

Fargo rose, 169, 174

featherstitch, 46, 47, 53, 105–24, 115, 134, 143, 174; illustrated instructions for, 111. *See also* beaded feather; bushes; drunken feather; fly stitch; maidenhair stitch; raining feathers; triple feather

floriography, 158

flowers, 4, 14, 22, 30, 32, 44, 46, 47, 63, 143, 158–71; bead flower and ribbon seam, 153; country rose, 161–62; Dupioni rose, 165; fantasy flower, 168–70; Fargo rose, 169, 174; folded-circle flower, 166–67; gathered flower, 158–59; pearl flower, 152; rolled roses, 163–64; velvet rickrack flower, 159–60; velvet yo-yo flower, 160; Victorian language of, 14. *See also* floriography; motifs

fly stitch, 66, 73, 105, 106–107, 109, 115, 136, 174; illustrated instructions for, 106, 107. *See also* featherstitch

focus fabric, 36, 37

foundation, 5, 42, 52; making, 35–36. *See also* muslin

French knot, 46, 65, 69, 71, 75, 78, 91, 96, 98, 100, 101, 102, 103, 104, 127, 130, 138–44, 156, 168, 169, 170, 174; illustrated instructions for, 139–40. *See also* pistil stitch

fringe, 154, 155

Godey's Lady's Book, 3, 11–13

goldwork, 16, 174

Good Housekeeping, 10–11

Grandmother's Fan, 19

Harper's Bazaar, 4

hardanger embroidery, 16, 174

hedebo, 16, 174

herringbone stitch, 55, 76–86, 88, 94, 99, 101, 102, 104, 126, 134, 174; illustrated instructions for, 77; interrupted, 79; tied, 46, 79, 80, 130. *See also* interlaced herringbone; shadow herringbone; twisted herringbone; woven herringbone

Homage to Ardelia, 26, 27–29

hoops, 52

interfacing, 30, 37

interlaced herringbone, 82–85, 174; illustrated instructions for, 84–85. *See also* herringbone stitch

Japanese aesthetics, 5

Japanese ceramics, 5, 7

Japanese ribbon stitch, 169, 175

Kensington stitch, 10, 61, 175; illustrated instructions for, 61

Kyle, Fred, 8, 9

lace, 13, 16, 19, 22, 31, 45, 46, 49, 107, 141, 146. *See also* bobbin lace; picot

layering, 4, 22, 23, 37, 42, 45, 121

lazy daisy, 46–47, 66, 67, 79, 80, 81, 87, 91, 92, 93, 98, 99, 101, 103, 125–26, 127, 128, 130, 131, 135, 136, 137, 141, 143, 152; illustrated instructions for, 125. *See also* bullion-tipped lazy daisy; chain stitch; decorated lazy daisy

maidenhair stitch, 110, 117–19; illustrated instructions for, 117, 118. *See also* featherstitch

magic chain, 130–32; illustrated instructions for, 130–31. *See also* chain stitch

motifs, 5, 16, 19, 20, 27, 28, 30, 32, 34, 36, 47, 51, 52, 54, 55, 58, 59, 60, 61, 63–64, 87, 107, 121, 141, 143, 146, 150; dragonfly, 151–52; floral, 63, 158; heart, 139, 163–64; sources of, 56; spiderweb, 64; star, 150. *See also* Dover Publications; flowers

Mountmellick work, 16, 175

muslin, 35–36, 41, 42, 45, 48, 52, 58. *See also* foundation

needlepoint, 16, 52, 53, 175

needles: choosing, 41–42, 51; threading, 56–57; types of, 52

needle tatting, 16, 175

New York Times, 8, 9–10

nook and cranny, 39, 42, 44, 175

or nué embroidery, 16, 175

outline stitch, 59, 60, 61, 175; illustrated instructions for, 61. *See also* stem stitch

pearls, 46, 82, 100, 101, 114, 123, 141, 145, 159, 160; flower, 152; seam treatment with, 157

Perchance, 23, 24, 25

picot, 28, 156, 175; illustrated instructions for, 156

pistil stitch, 143, 144, 170, 175; illustrated instructions for, 143. *See also* French knot

Proud as a Peacock, 17, 18, 22, 23
pulled thread, 16, 175

quilt blocks, 19, 20, 23, 27, 28, 30, 31, 35, 36, 48, 51, 55, 139, 146; piecing, 38–47

Rachel thread, 80, 91, 175
raining feathers, 110, 120, 132, 175. See also bushes; featherstitch
redwork embroidery, 59, 61, 175
Richelieu embroidery, 16, 175
rickrack, 154
Roses and Paisleys, 32, 33, 34

sampler work, 175
sashing, 22, 27, 30, 31, 175
satin stitch, 16, 23, 56, 139, 176
scrap quilt, 17, 176
sew and flip, 41, 43, 44, 176
shadow chevron, 46, 96, 176. See also chevron stitch
shadow herringbone, 82; illustrated instructions for, 82. See also herringbone stitch
shadow work, 16, 37, 68, 75, 176. See also shadow chevron; shadow herringbone
slip, 55
spiderwebs, 64
split stitch, 23, 176
stars. See motifs
State Historical Society of Missouri, 9
stem stitch, 27, 28, 46, 54, 59–64, 130, 134, 139, 152, 176; illustrated instructions for, 60. See also Kensington stitch; outline stitch; threaded stem stitch; whipped stem stitch
stencil, 55, 69, 71
straight seam, 16, 39, 43, 44, 48

straight stitch, 46, 58, 64, 66, 69, 73, 75, 79, 80, 91, 92, 94, 97, 98, 100, 101, 102, 103, 104, 126, 127, 129, 130, 132, 135, 153, 164, 169, 176
stumpwork, 16, 23, 176
surface embroidery, 16, 55, 175, 176

tack, 49, 57, 58, 89, 155, 164, 165
template, 41, 55, 160
tête de boeuf stitch, 136; illustrated instructions for, 136. See also chain stitch
thread: ending, 58; starting, 56–58; types of, 53–54, 59, 64
threaded stem stitch, 62, 176; illustrated instructions for, 62. See also stem stitch
tie-down stitch. See tying
transfers, 45, 53, 54–56; tools for, 54–55
triple feather, 110, 113–16; illustrated instructions for, 113, 116. See also featherstitch
twisted herringbone, 81, 143; illustrated instructions for, 81. See also herringbone stitch
tying, 4, 23, 27, 28, 31, 32, 126, 176

utility quilt, 22, 23

Victorian crazy quilts, 3–4, 8, 9, 10–14

whipped chain, 128; illustrated instructions for, 128. See also chain stitch
whipped stem stitch, 62, 176; illustrated instructions for, 62. See also stem stitch
whole cloth quilt, 23, 176
woven herringbone, 80. See also herringbone stitch

zigzag chain, 137. See also chain stitch